OVERCOMING IN BUSINESS AND LIFE

Wayland Coker has authored dozens of articles on entrepreneurship, business strategy, and management. He holds an MBA from George Washington University and is an accredited Certified Supply Chain Professional (CSCP). Retiring as a naval officer after over twenty years of service, including tours on a nuclear submarine during the Cold War, a surface ship during Operations Desert Shield and Desert Storm, and a Navy headquarters staff tour in the Pentagon, he started Coker Logistic Solutions (CLS).

OVERCOMING IN BUSINESS AND LIFE

A Common-Sense Playbook For Business Owners & Entrepreneurs

WAYLAND COKER

RUPA

Published by
Rupa Publications India Pvt. Ltd 2023
7/16, Ansari Road, Daryaganj
New Delhi 110002

Sales Centres:
Prayagraj Bengaluru Chennai
Hyderabad Jaipur Kathmandu
Kolkata Mumbai

Original English language edition published in 2022 by Koehler Books, 3705 Shore Drive, Virginia Beach Virginia 23455, USA. Arranged via Licensor's Agent: DropCap Inc.

P-ISBN: 978-93-5702-135-7
E-ISBN: 978-93-5702-136-4

First impression 2023

10 9 8 7 6 5 4 2 3 1

Printed in India

To my wife, Karen. Overcoming anything would be impossible without you.

Table of Contents

Introduction

"We should not look back unless it is to derive useful lessons from past errors, and for the purpose of profiting by dearly bought experience."

—George Washington

WAS THIS THE END?

I just sat there staring and staring for what seemed like hours. Lying on my desk in front of me were all the negative responses I had received from the many, many bank loan applications to finance the start of a new contract I had just won. It was a big contract, worth millions of dollars, that would put twenty-eight new people to work for my company. It was like a gift from heaven. My business was on the verge of collapse but now had renewed hope with this win. For the first time in months, I felt like I was going to make it. I hadn't had a significant contract win in several years. I was starting to feel optimistic for the first time in a long while.

My problem was, even with this new contract win, I still needed 120 days' worth of operating cash to finance the startup of the contract. There were salaries and other significant expenses to cover until the revenues from the client would start flowing. I'd never had trouble getting financing before, especially with a signed contract in hand. But this time, my primary bank told me no. My financial picture had indeed worsened over the last two years due to declining revenues from tighter markets and greater competition. So my bank was no longer willing to give me any more money.

But how was I supposed to get out of trouble if I wasn't allowed to win contracts, finance them, and work? I was stunned by their decision. I went looking elsewhere for funding, willing to consider almost anything: factoring, friends and family, investors. I even tried to take on a partner. But I couldn't get the money I needed. I could get a loan, but the interest rate quoted was so high it ate all my profits. You see, compounding my problem was that to win this contract, I had to bid extremely aggressively on price, giving me very low margins. My primary bank's interest rate would have worked fine if they had agreed to finance me with their usual interest rate. This was what I was counting on. But, as I said, they declined—even after I won the contract—and that rocked my world.

To add insult to injury, my relationship with my wife and kids was at an all-time low. I had allowed my business problems to overwhelm my personal life. My wife still loved me, of course, and I loved her dearly, but the tension that had developed between us was incredible. She was a full partner in our company; her name and signature appeared on all corporate documents, including the promissory notes with our primary business bank. She was just as financially exposed as I. We now argued more often over just about everything during these difficult months. It didn't need to be important, it just needed to be a thing—something, anything. As I write this, I can't recall any of the things we argued over; they were meaningless. We sometimes seemed to be in two different worlds. We were drifting apart. I know I was shutting her out, which is sometimes my way of coping with tragedy—going silent and becoming distant.

Beyond our business problems, she was also focused on keeping the home in a healthy routine, seeing to the needs of our three college-aged kids. I was focused on the business and its survival, not the family.

I was absent, physically and emotionally, from many family issues or events. The things she cared most about, I completely disregarded. And I don't mean to suggest that she was not aware of the business problems. She was. She often tried to talk to me about them, to offer support or encouragement. But I wasn't in the mood or didn't consider her opinion of much value. After all, I was the expert! Yeah, right. The truth is I got us into this mess all by myself. She was only guilty of trying to support me, to enable my dreams, to love me with all her heart. We allowed our business through the years to suck all the life out of our marriage, as well as our physical and mental well-being. I often felt I had nothing left to give. I felt we had no escape from this horror. My own self-loathing had never reached such intense levels. I could feel depression and a sense of loss settling over me, as I'm sure my wife did.

Yet even though the tension between my wife and me was incredible, I knew she and I were in this together, that our marriage would survive, that she would continue to love and support me and I would continue to love and support her. I had an unwavering assurance that regardless of how bad things got, she would never leave me. Our love would survive. I never doubted that. Never. It was that assurance that would later turn out to be the most important contributing factor to our subsequent recovery from this tragedy.

My children were aware of the situation yet gave me their unqualified support whenever the subject came up. They knew something was going on but didn't know how bad it had gotten. My wife and I tried to spare them the worry and pain by keeping them mostly out of it. I was ashamed at what was happening and what they might be thinking about their dad—a failure, poor decision-maker, not a good role model or provider. They never said this to me, but my own self-talk certainly did. I was going to have to tell two of my three kids that I no longer had money for college.

One of them had just graduated, so he was in the clear, but I felt so sorry and ashamed for the other two. My only daughter, a wonderful daughter whom I loved so much and was very proud of, was most likely going to marry the man she was dating, a young man whom we adored. How was I now going to afford to make her wedding an incredibly memorable day for her and the family? I had just spent a good deal of money on my oldest son's wedding a year earlier. He had married a wonderful young woman whom I love like my own daughter. But now my daughter deserved a great wedding, didn't she? What kind of dad was I if I couldn't give her the wedding she deserved? My only other son was still in college, working and living with us. He was a very talented young man who had hopes and dreams, too. How was I going to provide a college education for him?

I have to say again that through all of this, not once did any of my children condemn me, blame me, or express disappointment in me. To the contrary, my children would ask, "What can we do to help you, Dad?" Wow. It still brings tears to my eyes even now when I think of them and how they treated me. I really felt that I didn't deserve such children.

Our $3 million home was now unaffordable, and we stood to lose it. When I purchased the house, I had $1 million in equity that we had built up over twenty years of buying and selling our previous homes. But sadly, we bought our current home at the height of the housing bubble, and the market had now crashed and the equity was gone. My house was upside down. I owed more than it was worth, and I would not be able to keep up the payments. We tried unsuccessfully for two years to sell it, lowering the price again and again. My airplane would have to be sold. My forty-nine-foot sailing yacht would be repossessed since I owed more than it was worth. My Porsche, my Harley, and my wife's BMW would all have to be sold off.

With all of this, my problems were only just beginning. I owed a substantial amount of money to my primary business bank, a loan my wife and I had personally guaranteed, which is what you do as a small business owner. I also had an office lease that still had eighteen months left, totaling another substantial amount of money. To make matters worse, my landlord had a reputation for being very tough, and it was generally thought he would never release anyone from a lease, no matter the situation. I knew I would have to default on my office lease, and I could only imagine how hard he was going to make it for me.

Then there were my employees. Most of them had been with me for over sixteen years, worked tirelessly, believing in me, believing in the company and what we do. We'd been through so many peaks and valleys together. They all had families, mortgages, plans, hopes, dreams, and I was now going to repay all their hard work by laying them off? My partners and associates, who had stuck with me over the years, were now going to get a call from me saying that I was ceasing operations, that they would have to find someone else to do the jobs, to find someone else to fulfill the commitments I had made to them. They had been loyal to me, and now I was about to abandon them.

And what about my parents? They had been so proud of me. They were proud of their son, his solid marriage to a wonderful woman, his wonderful kids, a retired Navy veteran, MBA from a prestigious university, successful entrepreneur who had started a company that earned a spot on the Inc. 5000 list within a few short years, had been recognized as the 2012 Northrup Grumman Supplier of the Year out of thousands of suppliers, a yachtsman, an instrument-rated pilot, a jazz bassist, a lay minister in the church, and so on.

My parents, by example, had shown me how to live. They lived a life of honor, integrity, compassion, charity, and love of family. They always encouraged me to be my best, told me I could do anything I put my mind to do; they believed in me. They never had much money but did their very best to see I got the best opportunities possible. They loved me, and I felt it. But now their son was crashing and burning. All my life I wanted to please my parents, mostly because they were so good, and I wanted them to see that I was good enough to be their son, that their efforts had not been wasted on me. It now appeared to be a completely failed effort.

So I just sat there, staring at the neatly stacked pile of bank rejections. I felt myself sinking lower and lower into a dark state of depression after I realized it was over, at least for the US portion of my business, the biggest portion. I had no more contract opportunities or potential for work. I had exhausted all avenues for new business. Sure, there were other potential business targets, but they would take months, even years to develop, and I had no more time, financially. There was no more cash. There was no more US company.

How had this happened? How did I end up here with the world crashing around me? What perfect storm of events had brought me to the brink of disaster? Well, I was actually beyond the brink. This was a genuine disaster. I remember this was all a blur in my mind. I think when trouble like this comes, it is very hard to keep your perspective, to keep an eye on what's going on, to fully understand the elements at play around you—their relationships and potential impacts. It's all you can do to keep the ball in front of you, to keep focused on next steps, without trying to observe and make strategic sense of everything.

We small business owners are indeed very talented and able to handle many tasks, but even we have our limits. If some well-meaning person had tried to help me by giving me advice, or a good business book on strategy or leadership, I would have completely ignored it all. When you're in the storm, it's often hard to sit and let someone else give you sage advice—you're just trying to survive. What I needed most was someone to talk to, someone to listen, someone to empathize. The time for advice and counsel would come later—but not now.

Some months before, I came home to talk to my wife about our worsening financial picture and decided we needed legal advice. We were referred to a good attorney. We called him. We had been told by a close friend that most people wait too late to talk to an attorney and have few options left when the crisis really hits. Engaging early with an attorney often gives you more options. So our attorney was up to speed on our basic situation but didn't know the latest about all the rejection notices. Not knowing where to go from here, we sought his advice and again gave him a call.

After explaining our situation to him in detail and asking for his thoughts, our attorney paused, breathed deeply, and exhaled slowly. I could imagine him looking down at his papers with his forehead resting in one hand, the receiver in the other. He then probably lifted his head, looking straight ahead as he prepared to speak. He sounded very sad, even subdued. It was as if he were a doctor who was about to give me the worst news a doctor can give to mortal man. "It's over," he said. "I think we've done all we can. You've done all you can. There's no good option left. Our only course of action right now, I believe, is chapter 7. I'm very sorry, but you have to think about the future now and protecting yourself."

Bankruptcy! What? Had it really come to this? Tears filled my eyes. I looked at my wife, Karen, who had been trying to keep a positive face on all of this. But she now looked crestfallen. What must she think of me? What would my children think of me? What would my parents think of me? What would my faithful and loyal employees think of me? What would my friends and business associates think of me? What would my office landlord do to me? What would my bank do to me? Those were my friends. Oh my God! Was this really happening?

No, maybe I was just asleep and would soon wake up. I'd been having lots of restless nights with nightmares lately. Maybe this was just one of those episodes. I became very nauseated. But then, I'd been waking up most nights nauseated, dry-heaving for long periods, full of fear and torment, praying to God for divine intervention. This was one of the worst periods of my life. All my mental circuits were on overload. I had no words. I had no energy. I had no expression. I had nothing, just nothing. All I could do was sit there and stare out the window. Empty. Lifeless. Deep down, however, I knew our attorney was right.

Now what?

• • •

In the following days, weeks, months, and years, I did what I normally do after a setback—try to make some sense of a bad situation. This was my way, my habit, my character trait to look for the lesson, the meaning, to search for the silver lining and find a way to turn this around and make it work for my family and me. So I did some very honest and critical soul searching.

I took some time to recover emotionally from what had just happened and the shock of what our attorney had just advised. Then I began to consider that surely there must be more to life than pass or fail, success or defeat, prosper or decline. And what of failure; couldn't it also have a purpose if lessons learned were applied? I found myself sketching out in my journal what had happened, what might have been done differently even though much of what happened was unforeseeable. We were in the worst recession in decades, and it impacted the business horribly. I began to look for common threads, relationships, links between what worked and what did not. Even though much of what I had to deal with was out of my control, surely there were things I could have done differently that might have mitigated my situation and perhaps minimized my losses.

What had worked against me? What had worked for me? Who had worked against me? Who had worked for me? Was my business model outdated? Or was it fine and only needed some minor adjustments? And what could be done to prevent this kind of catastrophic demise from ever happening again?

These and many more questions sought answers and began informing my thinking. That was when I had the notion to write this book. I needed to write this book. I needed the therapy of writing all of this down, to pass it on and benefit my family and friends, but to also benefit anyone else who might be experiencing what I just went through—other business owners and entrepreneurs. I didn't want to waste this opportunity to help someone. I believe that we go through challenges to build our character and make us better people but also to inform and help others. This way of thinking put a new perspective and purpose on suffering in my mind—and this was very important to me. This book had to be written.

> ***"Thoughts disentangle themselves passing over lips and through pencil tips."***
>
> **—Anonymous**

As I began to journal about my experiences, which I have always tried to do because I think it brings clarity, I found several principles and ideas emerging. I discovered, looking at my notes in my journals, that I had been overly focused on the details of my crisis. I was missing the strategic view or "big picture." I was focusing on the trees instead of the forest. I needed a better perspective.

Over the next twelve to eighteen months, I began to consolidate and distill my thoughts. Several strategic and overarching ideas began to emerge, which I developed into principles that became the core concept and chapters of this book.

The core concept is the interdependency of your business and life, which I will explain in the next section. One affects the other, both negatively and positively, like an algebraic equation. This concept was something I wish I had fully understood or recognized when I was in the middle of my crisis. I mistakenly believed that if I had a good idea, worked really hard, was totally devoted to success, that would be enough to see me through whatever challenges got thrown my way. That assumption was not only wrong, it was harmful. I cannot say that I would have avoided my catastrophe if I'd understood and utilized these principles, but my response to it would have been much healthier, and I also believe the subsequent results would have been far less damaging and much better for my family and me.

You might be thinking, "This sounds like another work–life balance book." It is not. The most you can say is that it's a business–life balance book. Your typical work–life balance books, of which there are many, are written from an *employee's* perspective, NOT an *employer's* perspective. The perspectives are very different! Most employees leave the office or place of work and their worries stay at work. But for a business owner, work worries never leave. They stay with you all the time: at work, at home, even when you sleep. When you wake up, that eight-hundred-pound gorilla is still standing there, right in front of you, staring at you. You can't get away from it. So I get it. Being an employer, making payroll every two weeks, carrying all the risk, makes your problems very different from an employee. So what I have to say about it in this book is different.

This book is the book I needed when I was going through hell—a practical book. I didn't want an academic, overly technical, hard-to-read book. I wanted a playbook—something I could refer to when I found myself in certain situations! In American football language, I needed help with "What do I do on third and long? What do I do when my running game is not working? What play can I call?" I needed advice, options, and common sense. That's the kind of book I wrote—a playbook.

What I will do in the chapters that follow is fully explore this interdependency and give you the principles and wisdom I have learned. I'll finish by showing you how things have gone now that I've fully adopted these lessons and put them to use. Believe me, it has been a huge step in the right direction and has resulted in this book. Positive and wonderful things are happening again, and I have a sense of purpose I've not felt in a long while.

I believe as you read each chapter, you'll find ideas that will help you with your future challenges and opportunities, informing both your business and your life. But my greatest hope is that you'll also examine what you think you know. As Secretary of Defense, Donald Rumsfeld once said, "There are known knowns. These are things we know that we know. There are known unknowns. That is to say, there are things that we know we don't know. But there are also unknown unknowns. There are things we don't know we don't know." So, like Mr. Rumsfeld, I want to be prepared as best I can for the "unknown unknowns." Understanding the interdependence of your business and life will help you do just that.

I hope I have piqued your interest. I hope my story caused you to want to spend some personal time with me and see if my experiences or anything I have to say might be useful to you. If you're starting a new business, are already in business but struggling to survive, or maybe you're in business and just need some inspiration, come with me. I believe I can help. I want to share with you what I've learned and enable a better future for your business and life.

Let's get started.

PART ONE:

HOW DO YOU THINK?

CHAPTER ONE

The Interdependence and Balance of Your Business and Life

> *"More grass means less forest; more forest less grass. But either-or is a construction more deeply woven into our culture than into nature, where even antagonists depend on one another and the liveliest places are the edges, the in-betweens . . . relations are what matter most."*
>
> **—Michael Pollan**

I'M GOING TO ASSUME if you're reading this book that you're one of the many millions of entrepreneurs or small business owners out there working hard to realize your dream and that you're looking for advice and encouragement. Starting a new business or venture can be daunting, and there is so much to know. Or you might be looking for hope. Maybe you're going through an extremely difficult time, personally or professionally, and are hoping to find within the pages of this book someone who's experienced a similarly difficult situation and how they responded and emerged successfully. Or things may be going fine for you, but you worry that it could all come crashing down around you. You want to know if there's any way to prepare for the storm, what it looks like, and how to respond. If any of that describes you, then I think you've picked up the right book.

As you have read in the introduction, and as you will read throughout this book, it contains my stories, warts and all. Everything I hope to pass on to you has come from my personal experiences, things I went through, decisions I made and had to live with. I'm going to try to be real with you and speak plainly. I didn't make all the right decisions before, during, or after my crisis. But I did make enough right decisions, adjusting as I went. It was messy, but I learned a great deal. I hope you will see within these pages a flawed human being who lost it all but, through principles I will share with you, got back up and emerged healthy and thriving once again—a better version of myself. I hope you will be able to relate and see that you can not only survive but thrive, too. By no means do I claim to have all the answers, but I do believe I can help you. If you're in the pit of despair right now, like I was, I am here to encourage you. There is life after failure, after bankruptcy, after complete loss. In fact, from my own experience, there is a very good life awaiting you, if you learn the lessons and apply them to your life and business consistently. I also hope to help you avoid trouble, when possible. It's not always possible, but it's always better to be prepared. And if you're just starting out in business, then this book may be one of the best primers you'll find on what may lie ahead.

Understanding Balance and Interdependence

I'd like to begin this first chapter by discussing the concept of balance as it relates to the interdependence between your business and life. First let's establish an understanding of the word *balance*.

One common definition of the word balance is "an even distribution of weight enabling someone or something to remain upright and steady."[1] This is a pretty good definition for the purposes of this book. We definitely want to remain upright and steady, and I love the notion from this definition that we need an "even distribution of weight" in order to remain upright and steady. Keep this in mind as we move on.

Without realizing it, we experience the idea of balance all the time. We go throughout our daily lives encountering things that are constantly moving in and out of balance. Our automobile tires may start out in balance after a visit to the shop, but after several thousand miles of driving and the occasional pothole, our tires get out of balance and start to vibrate. It's really annoying, not to mention it increases our fuel and maintenance costs. If you've ever picked up two suitcases, one much heavier than the other, the load is quite uncomfortable and much harder to carry than suitcases more evenly weighted. Or have you ever picked up a long, thin object such as a two-by-four? You wouldn't try to pick it up from one of the ends; you'd go to the center of the board and pick it up. It's much easier to manage when you carry a balanced load. Or how about a bicycle? If you don't keep yourself evenly balanced as you ride, making turns, stopping, and starting off, you'll find yourself on the ground very quickly. If you want to reach your destination, you have to keep it balanced.

And it's not just the physical world where we encounter balance issues. In our work life, we can find ourselves spending too much time on one task, ignoring other tasks, creating tension for us with our coworkers or clients. We can eat too much of one kind of food, rather than a balanced diet, and our bodies will suffer from its effect. We can spend too much time with the wrong kind of people, such as those who are overly negative, lazy, small-minded, self-centered, and we will likely feel the negative effects in our mind and attitude. Or if we don't balance work and rest properly, we will start to feel the negative consequences in our bodies and our performance. I can safely say that too much of almost anything, even things we love, usually carries negative consequences for us. There may be rare exceptions, like air.

---

1 New Oxford American Dictionary

But you could argue that too much air too quickly can cause you to hyperventilate. So even air can be overdone, too. Let's just agree that balance, in almost everything in life, is better than imbalance.

The word *interdependence* is commonly defined as "the state of being dependent upon one another: mutual dependence."[2] Just like balance, we see this kind of thing all the time, too.

In nature we see a good example of interdependence between the termite and the protozoa. Protozoa live in the termites' stomachs and break down the cellulose from the wood the termites eat. Without the cellulase protozoa produce to break down the cellulose in wood into sugar that termites can absorb through their stomachs, termites would starve. Protozoa benefit from the termites by receiving food and shelter.[3] They are interdependent. They need each other to survive.

We see interdependence in business. Manufacturers produce things that people need and consumers buy—clothing, for example. Without consumers, manufacturers could not continue to operate, and consumers wouldn't get the things they need. Each is interdependent on the other. They each benefit from each other.

Debunking the Notion of a Separate Personal and Professional Life

I'd like to challenge the notion so often heard in professional circles that "I keep my personal and professional life separate and distinct. I can't let one interfere with the other." If you Google "keeping your personal and professional life separate," you'll find literally hundreds and thousands of articles on how to do this. I've read many of them. These are well-meaning people, I'm sure. However, my experience has shown YOU CANNOT SEPARATE YOUR PERSONAL AND PROFESSIONAL LIFE. I was not able to do it, nor will you be able to do it, in my opinion. So don't try.

2 https://www.merriam-webster.com/dictionary/interdependence
3 https://prezi.com/z_u_-ccp0nyn/termites-and-protozoa/

What happens at work leaks into and affects your personal life. What happens in your personal life leaks into and affects your professional life. It's just that simple. To suggest that you can somehow isolate these two important parts of life and keep them from interacting and influencing each other is not only wrong but harmful. They must be managed together to give you the greatest opportunity to live at your best and for your highest purpose.

I do believe in setting boundaries in your life, at work, at home, and with any other personal pursuits. But having healthy boundaries does not conflict with the notion that your personal and professional lives are interdependent. Setting boundaries, to my way of thinking, is actually the process of acknowledging your life and business are interdependent and must be managed together so they each work better for you. You can't manage your life like you manage your business; they are not the same, but they must be managed together if they are to stay in balance. You have a home and you live there. It is different from your office where you work. They are separate, but interdependent. You work to pay for the home, and your home is where you rest so you can work. Do you see? Your home and work have their own boundaries and are separate, but they are interdependent.

The bigger question is how well are they integrated? Let me give you an example. A few years ago, if you visited my home to watch a movie with us, you would have seen an audio-visual system that was the most complicated, difficult, and bug-prone system ever. I had one brand of television, another brand of DVD player, another brand of CD player, another brand of cable and internet access boxes, all connected to another brand of sound system. It worked, usually. But switching back and forth between boxes, using a multitude of remote controls, or trying to record with one unit while another was playing was a fool's errand. It was laughable and embarrassing, especially when your guests were watching you struggle. To be sure, the pieces were all integrated and all connected. I mean, I could eventually get the sound and video out that I wanted, but it was onerous and tiresome. You needed a graduate degree to operate it.

However, if you visit my house now, you'll see only a television, a sound system, and cable and Apple TV boxes. I switch easily between them. I only need one remote. I get whatever content I want, when I want. The sound is awesome. The video is awesome. And I find I can do new things all the time since the software is constantly being improved and upgraded by a manufacturer who cares. That's what true integration looks like: separate pieces working well together. Again, my old system was indeed integrated, just not very well. Your life and business are integrated, at least by default, but they may not be integrated well. The better they are integrated, the better each will work, giving you the best results.

So that's all well and good, assuming everything works. What happens when one of the system boxes breaks? It usually affects the entire system. If the sound system broke, the whole thing was affected, and I could only use the video system. If the television broke, then I was stuck with only audio capability. My point is that the whole system is degraded when one part breaks. If you accept that your life and business are integrated, you also have to accept that when something happens in one part, it affects the other part—much like an algebraic equation, where what happens on one side of the equation affects the other. When something at work goes wrong, it will affect your personal life, and vice versa. We can't help it. We're human beings and are susceptible to our emotions, our instincts, and our fears. We have the uncanny ability to imagine all sorts of outcomes when things go wrong.

How many times have you had a tragic event at work and when you got home, it was still there in your mind, affecting your emotions? You didn't just leave it at work. You couldn't. How did you get along with those at home afterward? If you're like me, you may have interacted with your family or friends without using your best and highest version of yourself—maybe like a grumpy old cuss. You may have been short, argumentative, or reclusive. And the same thing can happen when we have a tragic event at home. When we go into work the next day, we can't always just leave the event at home.

We do our best, sure. But it does impact our emotions, our thinking, our performance at work.

What we want is to learn as much as we can about the link between your business and your life, how they are connected, how they influence each other, and how to best manage them together in order to thrive. That old audio-video system example I mentioned earlier was composed of pieces built separately, by separate companies who had competing ideas about how their box should work. When you put all the many boxes together, the result was a clunky, hard-to-use system that did not deliver the best experience. The new system was designed to be managed together, to be easy to use, and to be continually improved—more able to handle future demands for our entertainment. Wow! Things work much better when they are created, built, and managed in an integrated way.

The Balance and Interdependence Model

Having now established that your life and business, or professional life, are connected and cannot be separated, we need to understand how they are connected. What is the relationship between your life and your business? How does one affect the other? What does balance or imbalance look like? How are they interdependent? So, let's break it down.

When I refer to your life, I am referring to your personal life, everyone and everything about you that is not work or business related. I am talking about that part of your life that includes your relationships, such as family and friends, those you spend your leisure time with, those you pursue charitable activities with, those who love you and/or care about you, the person. These are the people with whom you share your heart, your important personal events, even those with whom you worship. I am also talking about how you spend your leisure time—hiking, camping, reading, participating in a sports activity, theater, concerts, shopping, anything you do to unwind or enjoy your life.

When I refer to your business, I am referring to your work or professional life, everything you do to make a living that supports your personal life. If you own a business, this will include all activities needed to establish, grow, and maintain your business. This includes all activity to manage employees, manage clients or customers, marketing, financial management, networking, professional social activity, professional or trade organizations, and any further education or training you take to enhance your business.

What you must understand, and fully accept if you are to benefit from this book, is that your life and business are interdependent. What does that mean? For our purposes, it means things that rely on each other for their survival or day-to-day existence. Taking this a bit further, Nicolay Worren tells us that interdependencies exist[4] when actions in one sub-unit of an organization affect important outcomes in another sub-unit. If the manufacturer in my example above changes its product line to something other than clothing, the consumer will spend money elsewhere to get the needed clothing. If the consumer decides different clothing is needed and goes elsewhere to get it, the manufacturer is impacted by dropping demand for its clothing. If either the manufacturer or consumer changes its behavior related to the clothing, it affects the other. They are interdependent.

It is the very same idea when you consider your business and your life—they are interdependent. One needs the other. One affects the other. They cannot be separated.

In the study of economics, the interdependency concept says that all prices are to some degree affected by all other prices and also that all markets are affected by all other markets.[5] One affects the other. You see this all the time in the stock market, at a fish market, or in a location where there are several gasoline stations within eyesight of each other. When one drops a price, they all tend to drop it. Or

4 Worren, Nicolay (2012. *Organisation Design: Re-defining complex systems.* Pearson.

5 The New Dictionary of Cultural Literacy, Third Edition

when fuel shortages occur, it usually occurs market-wide, and together they raise prices. This concept of interdependency permeates life and business in countless ways.

In the case of our business and personal lives, they are interdependent because they need each other to exist. I need my business to provide me financial resources so I can support my personal life, and my business needs me to run and operate it. Each needs the other to exist. Going further using Worren's notion, when my business suffers, thereby reducing the amount of financial support it can provide to me, that affects my personal life. What happens to one affects the other, and it goes both ways.

To help us further understand this concept, I've created a simple graph (see figure 1) to represent the relationship between your life and your business.

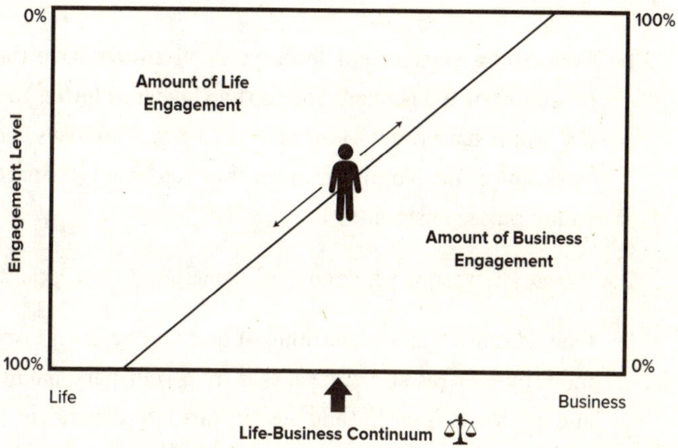

To orient your eyes to this graph, let me explain the various elements of it. On the vertical or Y axis is the engagement level expressed as a percentage. Notice this goes from 0 to 100 percent starting from top to bottom. The vertical axis on the right side goes from 0 to 100 percent but from bottom to top. *Engagement Level* is meant to represent how much effort or commitment, in time and resources, you are spending in a particular area. I'll have more on this later.

The X axis is what I call the *Life-Business Continuum*, with *Life* on the extreme left and *Business* on the extreme right. This axis is meant to represent where you are in terms of the balance between your life and business. If you're spending more time on life pursuits, then you are at a point somewhere on the left-most side of the axis. If you're spending more time on business pursuits, then you're at a point somewhere on the right-most side of the axis.

Dissecting the entire box into two equal halves is the line that is meant to represent the combination of your engagement level as it relates to your life and business. The little human figure is you, and can move freely along the diagonal line to represent where you are in terms of your balance between your life and business.

Some principles or ground rules to remember as we use this graph:

1. Concerning engagement level, you will always have the constraint of 100 percent. You can't go higher or lower. You will always have twenty-four hours in a day, seven days in a week, and so on. Nothing changes this. You have to manage within those constraints.

2. You are always somewhere on the diagonal line. No exceptions.

3. One side always affects the other. When your business takes more time or resources, it takes it from your personal life and vice versa. Your life and business are interdependent.

4. You'll note the diagonal line, at its most extreme right and left ends, goes to near 100 percent on the life engagement level (left side of the diagonal line), and near 100 percent at the business engagement level (right side of the diagonal line). This is meant to suggest that sometimes our lives and businesses do require all of our time and resources. This should

be temporary, but this attribute will allow us to discuss those extreme moments in an entrepreneur's life where exceptional effort is required, whether in life or business.

5. And finally, the goal of every entrepreneur and business owner is to keep themselves somewhere in the middle one-third of the model's area, as near to 50 percent for both life and business as possible. This would represent a target for healthy equilibrium.

Note that as you move up and down the continuum's diagonal line, your engagement level is always equal to 100 percent. When you spend more time on your business, you are taking more time from your personal life, and vice versa. Consider a glass that is half full of water. What else is in the glass? Air, of course. So, actually, the glass is full. As you drink more water, that volume is replaced with more air. As you add more water, air is displaced by the water. Sometimes it has no water and all air. Other times it has all water and no air. Most of the time it has some of each, like our lives. We sometimes must focus on our businesses 100 percent of the time. Sometimes our lives require all of our attention. But mostly, our engagement level is a mixture of life and business. Just remember our lives are always equal to 100 percent. We are always fully engaged.

Your Life and Business Must Be Managed Together

I'm hopeful by now that you understand my notion that there is a direct relationship between your life and business. Because I believe they are so connected, one affecting the other, I want to suggest to you that it's better if they are managed together rather than separately.

Try to imagine, if you can, that you are responsible for leading and managing a military unit. Let's say this unit is made up of one hundred soldiers, men and women trained for combat anywhere in the world. This is obviously a big responsibility, to lead our country's most treasured resource, its men and women. Of course, you want to make sure you do the job properly.

As a former military officer, let me say there are many, many things you have to think about. But for purposes of our discussion, we're only going talk about two things you need to consider to do the job properly:

1. preparing the soldiers for their mission, and
2. making sure they have all the things they need for the mission—or their support.

You've been given the mission by the Headquarters Command. It will require your soldiers to have certain skills. Your soldiers can do it, no problem, but some training is required before they're ready. So you schedule the right instructors and schools for them. They're going to be operating in a very hot environment, so their training needs to prepare them for operations in those conditions. They're going to need to use new pieces of equipment, new technologies they've not used before, so they'll need to build some expertise using it. They will also need to prepare to be away from their homes and families for many months, so they each need to get their personal lives in order. This is important so their attention is focused on the mission and they're not distracted with worries about things at home.

Next, you start thinking about the support needed to accomplish this mission. As you can imagine, your soldiers are going to need all kinds of support. At the moment, they are currently being supported very well. They are at their home military base, living with their families, doing routine training of various types to stay sharp and maintain a baseline of preparedness for their duties. They get their food from a mess hall if they live in the barracks or from a grocery store if they live at home. They get their training from well-established providers of training. They have everything they need. Everything's in balance.

> ***"The point is the unit and the support of the unit have to be managed together, just like your personal and professional life."***

But things will now change, and the problem is you can't send the soldiers on this new mission using the same support they are getting now in routine conditions. In other words, you cannot manage their support separately from their mission. It has to be done together. The support must change to match the mission. If you don't match the support to the mission, they won't get what they need, they won't be prepared, and they will fail the mission, probably putting lives in jeopardy. No one wants that. The point is the unit and the support of the unit have to be managed together, just like your personal and professional life. It's important that we all understand that our lives and businesses are interdependent and must be kept in balance.

Which Is More Critical to Get Right—Business or Life?

The last point I want to make in this chapter is perhaps the most important. Of the two subjects—business and life—which one is more critical to do right, to manage well? If I only consistently get one of them right, which one must it be? Which one has more impact? Of course, we want to do them both well, but does one carry more influence than the other?

The short answer is yes. If you only do one of them right consistently, you want it to be life. Show me a situation where an entrepreneur's life is in total chaos over a long period, but her business is running extremely well, and I'll show you a business that is at risk of failure. On the other hand, show me an entrepreneur whose business is struggling, but her personal life is strong where she is well loved, and I'll show you a business that will most likely survive and go on to thrive.

“ . . . show me an entrepreneur whose business is struggling, but her personal life is strong and she is well-loved, and I’ll show you a business that will most likely survive and go on to thrive.”

This was my situation. My business had hit the wall, but my personal life and support system was strong. I emerged stronger with a much better, much more sustainable business. Reverse the situation, strong business but unhealthy personal life, and the results are not as promising. I’ve seen this time and time again. It’s best that both your life and business are healthy, but of the two, the health of your personal life is more critical. Please remember that.

Throughout the rest of the book, I will be discussing this and more as I give you the hard-won lessons and wisdom I’ve learned with advice you can use—a playbook. I believe it can help you.

PRINCIPLE 1

Your business and life are interdependent, one affecting the other, and must be kept in balance.

CHAPTER TWO

The Power of an Idea

"Believe in yourself! Have faith in your abilities! Without a humble but reasonable confidence in your own powers, you cannot be successful or happy."

—Norman Vincent Peale

WHEN YOU SEE THE word *power* or *powerful*, what comes to mind? Maybe some will think of a giant sperm whale or grizzly bear. Some will think of Mother Nature's power in the form of a hurricane, tornado, or typhoon. Others will think of large machines like the massive container ships that sail our seas, or the lethal aircraft carriers that patrol the world's oceans, or the impressive space shuttles we've seen rocket into space. Sports enthusiasts might focus on a favorite baseball player and his powerful home-run swing, a professional linebacker on an American football team that can deliver a devastating blow, the same for a prop on a rugby team, an Olympic weight lifter, or Usain Bolt, who was once the fastest man alive. Of course, all of those answers would be good examples of power, each in their own way.

But I'm willing to bet most people won't think that *ideas* are perhaps one of the most powerful things known to man. One could argue that Mother Nature and our natural universe can offer more powerful things than man-made ideas, but you have to admit we only know about the power of Mother Nature and the universe because of these powerful things called ideas. Someone had to think of these powerful forces, study them, understand them, name them, and then teach it all to us so we'd know what to call them and how to respect them.

Look around you. Practically everything you see started out as someone's idea. A chair, a table, paper, ink, books, language, writing, medicine, and on and on. Your mobile phone that has access to the whole of man's knowledge, right in your pocket! An amazing idea!

Alexander Graham Bell had an idea; now we have the phone. Louis Pasteur had an idea; now we have the ability to vaccinate people against disease and to drink pasteurized milk, avoiding food poisoning. Leonardo da Vinci had an idea; now we have mechanical looms and hydraulic saws. Thomas Edison had an idea; now we have the light bulb. Benjamin Franklin had an idea; now we have bifocal lenses. Bill Gates and Steve Jobs both had tons of ideas; now we have personal computers and personal digital assistants. How did we ever live without them? Then there's Henry Ford and the mass manufacturing processes he started that made automobiles affordable and available to everyone.

Think about whoever invented the first wheel. Can you imagine life without the wheel? What about the airplane? What about air-conditioning? Each summer when I walk from the hot and humid weather into my cool home, I thank God for Willis Carrier, the inventor of the air conditioner. Life today would not exist as we know it without the free flow of ideas and our ability to bring them to life.

Unfortunately, there are also many examples of people who had dangerous and harmful ideas. Think about all the horrible results of the ideas of Adolf Hitler, Vladimir Lenin, Benito Mussolini, Joseph Stalin, Idi Amin, and Saddam Hussein, to name just a few.

The last example I'll offer of a powerful idea is America itself. Alexis de Tocqueville, a Frenchman, set out to analyze American culture and politics, which resulted in his 1835 published book called

Democracy in America. In his book, Tocqueville revealed he believed that equality was the great political and social idea of his era, and he thought that the United States offered the most advanced example of equality in action. He was critical of many things in America, including the irony of this great American social idea combined with the treatment of Native Americans and the embrace of slavery.[6] But overall it was this *idea* of America that he found so powerful, for that is what America really is—a powerful idea. And in a relatively short period of time America has become the most powerful, influential country in the world—from an idea.

What About Your Idea?

I hope you now agree that ideas are powerful things. So, whatever your idea is, whether for your business or other purposes, it has power. Do not allow yourself to belittle or depreciate your idea. I've talked to so many would-be entrepreneurs who seemed to have very exciting and practical ideas, only to hear them say, "But it probably won't work," or "Someone else has probably already done this," or "No one would pay for this." Their idea hasn't even got out of the starting gate and they've killed it already!

The sad truth is that for every good idea that makes it to market or gets into the hands of the person that really needs the idea, there are many that did not even make it out of the entrepreneur's head. Have you ever watched something unfortunate happen in front of you and say, "Someone should really do something about that," or "Someone should invent something that fixes that problem"? I know I have. Of course, I can no longer remember the idea I had when I said that—I should have written it down—and I'm sure there are ideas that I've tossed aside that would've been very useful to society if I could have brought them about. It's shameful, really. We entrepreneurs ought to be better stewards of our brain power, our creativity, and our

6 http://www.history.com/topics/alexis-de-tocqueville

imaginations. It really is a gift, and I want you to see it just that way—a gift to be cherished and to be used to help our fellow man.

To be sure, not every idea will be worthy of your full effort to bring it to reality. That's not physically possible or practical. So how does one know when he or she has an idea that is worthy of consideration? Which ideas should be considered seriously? Which should be tossed aside or at least filed away to be used later to inform our thinking?

The best way I know to answer that question is to ask you how you felt when you first had that idea. Did you get excited? Did your brain go into overdrive? Did you begin to see this becoming a reality in your mind? When you described it to your spouse, friends, or associates, did they respond like you and say, "Wow! That would be amazing. That's a great idea!" Did you lie awake that night, and many nights afterward, thinking about your idea? Did you see yourself making this idea happen? Time will tell if this idea is worthy of your time and consideration. If you still feel as strongly about this idea days or weeks later as you felt on day one, that's a big clue that this could be an idea worth working on.

Another clue would be to ask yourself, "What problem would my idea solve? Who would it help?" Aren't you glad the inventors and creative thinkers I mentioned earlier, who brought positive change to our way of life, didn't just sit on their ideas? Millions of people have benefited from their ideas. And your idea doesn't have to be a new vaccine, or a breakthrough in agricultural technology that will greatly reduce world hunger, or have the potential for any other massive global impact. It could be something small but useful. Think about the lowly paper clip. The world could do without them, but aren't they extremely useful?

Some ideas are in the realm of advice or counsel rather than physical things. Think about the great book *How to Win Friends and Influence People* by Dale Carnegie. I saw a report that showed it has sold over thirty million copies. It was first published in 1936 and is still selling today. It gives practical advice for people dealing with everyday life—one of the greatest self-help books ever written. Mr. Carnegie had a clear idea of who he wanted to help. So, ask yourself, "Who will my idea help?" That will drive much of how you approach your idea and its path to reality.

Alternatively, if the idea does not excite you, stir your mind, or alter your emotions, I don't think you would have the requisite level of commitment needed to see the idea through to reality. If there is no passion in you for this idea, it's not going to get your best and highest effort or energy. How do you know if you have enough passion for the idea? If you have to ask that question, you've already answered it: you don't. The passion will come; it will be inherent, automatic. You'll have no problem getting excited about it at all. There will be no mistaking your passion. Now match that passion with competency, planning, and a balanced personal life to support your efforts, and you are well on your way to a happy result.

By the way, if you find yourself having trouble getting any ideas, or thinking beyond your initial idea, maybe you're just in a slump and need a little push to get going. There are things you can do to get your creative juices flowing, such as read a novel by a favorite author, go for a long walk in a visually beautiful place, see a fabulous movie or play, listen to your favorite music or go to a concert, talk to someone who is close to you, talk to someone who you know is creative, watch a cooking show, get some sleep, get some exercise, but do something that makes you happy or feel good. Chances are one of these things will start the creative flow.

Make Sure It's Your Idea

Another important thing I'll say concerning choosing your idea is to make sure it's your idea. The last thing you need as you start to succeed with your business idea is for someone to come knocking on your door, wanting a piece of the business because they think you stole their idea. This has happened to entrepreneurs before, and it is a depressing and difficult thing to deal with. Ask yourself where you got your idea. Did it come to you in a dream, while reading a book, while singing in the shower, while watching others struggle with a problem? Or did it come from a conversation with someone else while they were telling you their own ideas? If you need legal counsel on this point, I would seriously consider it.

In my case, my business idea was to take someone else's idea, improve it, then market it. Sound dangerous? It could have been, but I built a vibrant small business with contracts in four different countries and over fifty employees based on this idea. What if the person who first had the idea came to me after I had hit my peak and said, "Okay, Wayland. Great job building this business. Now share the wealth or I'll sue! You took my idea!" That would have been a disaster.

But it never happened. Why? Before I got started, I spoke with the man who had the first idea. You need to know that he had abandoned the idea because he had failed to make it successful. However, I saw what he did and thought it was good but needed some significant improvements. I approached him and told him I liked his idea. I told him I had plans to improve it and wanted to market it. I asked if he would have any objections. I did not offer him a share in the business because I felt my improved idea was so different from the original, and the costs involved in marketing significant enough, that this established the new and improved idea as my own. But I also felt it a wise move to try to get his agreement so that he would not attempt to make a claim against me in the future over the business.

He said he had no objections and even added that if I could get the idea successfully off the ground, then I deserved whatever rewards came with it. He also told me he thought "it was a waste of time, but good luck anyway." I never heard from him again. I know that he did learn of my success later because I was privy to a conversation between him and a friend about me and my success. He had nothing but kind things to say about me and wished me well. Unfortunately, he passed away soon after that conversation was relayed to me.

My situation was not so unusual, by the way. Many entrepreneurs enter the market offering new products and services that very often are not their own, or they were not the inventor or originator of the first idea. What frequently happens is that the first inventor or originator is unable to get to market with his or her idea. They are very knowledgeable and skilled in their areas of expertise, but they often lack the very different set of skills required to monetize their idea. This happens a lot. So your idea doesn't need to be originally yours, but you should take careful steps to ensure there will be no claims against you if you're successful, as I did.

What Does an Idea Need?

> ***"First comes thought; then organization of that thought, into ideas and plans; then transformation of those plans into reality. The beginning, as you will observe, is in your imagination."***
>
> **—Napoleon Hill**

So now you've got an idea—one that really excites you and solves a real problem. How next to proceed? My wife and I like to go hiking. Before we go, however, we prepare. We get our backpacks together, load them with appropriate food and water, first-aid kits, dry clothing, a compass, and other essentials. Why? Because if our definition of success is to have fun doing this hiking idea, those are the things we will need to be successful. I would not have fun on this hike without water, or without healthy food or snacks to keep up my energy, or if I got lost because I had no compass. This hiking idea needs certain things to succeed.

It's the same with your business idea or other creative venture. It will need certain things to succeed, things that will cultivate it and set the conditions for a successful journey to reality. What are those things? A good idea generally needs a healthy owner, commitment, faith, patience, definition, competencies, resources, and a market.

Each idea will need different things, but I'm going to address this list of things I believe are common to most all ideas. I put them in order of priority. Please pay attention to the order. You will need to add or modify this list to fit your situation.

1. Healthy Owner. The most important thing a new idea needs is an owner who is healthy. What do I mean by healthy? Does your life have to be perfect and everything about your life in order? No, not at all. But if your idea is going to survive the challenges that it will undoubtedly face, and if the owner isn't in a healthy place in their personal lives, everything will be put at greater risk. The owner needs a strong support system of relationships, people that are close to him or her and can speak freely into their lives and situations. An owner needs truthful feedback, honest and candid discussion, helpful advice and counsel. An owner should not be in the middle of a life crisis—a messy divorce, a recent death of a loved one, a body battling debilitating sickness or disease. All of these things will distract and put the idea at greater risk. The owner of the new idea needs to be in a good productive routine and must maintain that routine even when pressures from life or from launching the idea come, and come they will. They must not allow their lives to get out of balance, with the business bringing an imbalance to their personal lives or vice versa. Every effort must be made to keep business and life in balance. I allowed myself to get out of balance a few times in my situation, and I know I did not get the best and highest results I could have gotten. Do please note that I've placed this need at the top of the list. It is number one for a reason. Keep your body, your mind, and your spirit in good health. It is absolutely essential not only to your success but to your happiness. As I stated in the last chapter, your personal life's health is more critical to your success than your business's health.

2. Commitment. There is often a very fine line between success and failure in business and life. Your level of commitment to your idea can tip the scales in your favor, just as your lack of commitment can destroy it. Once when I was at a mountain lodge, as part of a professional retreat, we were rounded up and taken on a treetop adventure. We were asked to climb, balance, and zip-line our way through a treetop obstacle course about twenty to twenty-five feet off the ground. There were many very creative obstacles on this course that we had to navigate and conquer in order to complete the course. There was no ladder down to the ground. The only way down was to finish successfully. Of course, if there had been an injury, our guides would have rigged up lines to lower us to the ground. But beyond that, there was no quick or obvious way down once we started the course.

   Several of the obstacles were very challenging for me, but there was one in particular that I thought impossible. It contained about a dozen four-by-four-inch wooden fenceposts individually hanging vertically from a cable, freely swinging back and forth, with foot pegs at the bottom of each post. We were supposed to go from post to post, stepping from foot peg to foot peg while clutching the post close to our chests, and while everything was swinging back and forth. There was nothing stable to stand on or grasp. It was horrible, and I was not doing well. In fact, I started the obstacle two times and stepped back onto the safety of the platform each time as fear overcame me. If there had been a ladder nearby, I would have ended my adventure right there. But as I said, there was no convenient way down.

   The guide watching from the ground, sensing I was struggling, came over and gave me some verbal instructions to help me. His instructions seemed sensible, but as I started to try again, my confidence wasn't any better. But I tried moving from just one post to the next using his instructions. It worked. It was hard, but it worked. When I looked ahead at the next ten posts, all swinging back and forth, I knew I had to dig deep. I again was tempted to get off that obstacle but soon found that now that I knew the technique, I began to believe I could do it. I did do it, very slowly but successfully. A cheer went up behind me as my friends encouraged me, and they later told me how impressed they were that I overcame my fear and pushed on.

Actually, it was more a decision about the commitment that I made. Once the guide told me what to do, the fear subsided. Since I had no way down, I realized I was committed and had no choice but to push on.

"Yes, I did need some instruction, but it was the commitment that got me to the other side."

Yes, I did need some instruction, but it was the commitment that got me to the other side. Your business idea will need your commitment. Don't give yourself a "ladder down." In your mind, you must set your goals firmly and not abandon the idea when things get tough. If you need it, get some advice or instruction, like I did. It did help. But I still had to complete the obstacle myself. Remember, when Cortez got to the new world, he burned his ships. With no way back, Cortez knew his crew would not be tempted to abandon the idea of settling the new world but instead be fully committed to its success.

3. Faith. There have been volumes and volumes written on this subject, yet I feel there is still a need for clarity. For most people, this is a tough subject to understand. Let me try to simplify it. When I talk about faith, I'm talking about belief.

Most people think they don't have much faith, or they think you either have it or you don't. Nothing is further from the truth. Maybe you're thinking, "How can I tell if I have faith?" Have you ever been afraid or felt fear? I'm sure you have. Maybe during a time in your life when you experienced fear, your heart raced, your breathing got faster, you broke out in a sweat, maybe your sleep was affected, and so on. It was real, right?

Let's define the fear you were feeling as "believing something's going to happen." That's what you were doing when you were afraid, right? Nothing has happened yet, but you believed strongly that something was going to happen. But now let's consider faith. Turns out we can also define it as "believing something's going to happen." Wait. Wasn't that the same definition for fear? Yes, and that's my point. Fear is faith in reverse. Fear is negative, faith is positive. Both are about believing something that hasn't happened yet! Are you with me? If you have experienced fear, that's proof you have faith or the ability to believe—you believe something is going to happen that hasn't happened yet. So, in my view, faith is a positive belief, fear is negative belief.

We all start with the same amount of faith, but some of us put it to work, some of us don't. And just like the negative symptoms you experienced when you were afraid, you can have positive symptoms of faith, too. When you truly believe in your idea, these symptoms will appear; you get happy thinking about it, your heart races, you daydream, your sleep is affected, you see it all working in your mind's eye, you smile, you laugh, and so on. Do you believe in your idea? Do you believe in yourself? Do you believe in those around you who are committed to your idea, too? You have to be totally convinced about your idea. There can be no doubt. If there is doubt, others will notice it in your presentations, your body language, and your messaging.

I believe faith is like a muscle; so how can we grow stronger in our faith? Just like a muscle, you have to exercise it. Your faith in your idea will grow stronger as you get more experience, as you stay around positive people who speak encouragement, as you use your imagination and "see" the idea as a reality in your life, as you hear other success stories and are encouraged by them, and as you develop strong healthy relationships with those you love and care about.

4. Patience. It seems that in our modern world, patience is a virtue in short supply. We want things quickly, which often prevents us from fully realizing our dreams. During a Sunday sermon I heard recently, one of my pastors spoke about the characteristics of a type of bamboo that grows in Anji County in China. It can take five years before any growth is seen. During these five long years, the seeds have to be watered faithfully each day, with no visible signs of progress. Just imagine that. How many of us would be tempted to quit? Then, when it finally sprouts and begins growing, in just six weeks it can grow to over ninety feet tall.

   Bamboo, considered by the Chinese as one of the "Four Gentlemen" (bamboo, orchid, plum blossom, and chrysanthemum), plays such an important role in traditional Chinese culture that it is even regarded as a behavior model of the gentleman—one of those behaviors being patience. If you don't give the bamboo time to grow but uproot it when you don't see anything happening, you destroy its potential. It's the same with your idea. It will need adequate time to mature, to prove itself, to show its value. Many ask me, "What should I be doing while I'm patiently waiting for my idea to succeed?" Good question. Do the daily things that will make your idea a reality; as with the Chinese bamboo, it needed daily watering for five years. Ignore those who say it cannot happen. Push past your own fear and keep taking action.

Leo Tolstoy once said, "The two most powerful warriors are patience and time." I want you to notice Tolstoy used the word *warriors*. We often think that waiting is doing nothing. That's not true. When you are patiently waiting, you are deliberately doing something. When you show patience, you are behaving like a warrior in your fight to succeed. See your patience as a proactive step. Give your idea time to develop, like the Chinese bamboo. You might ask, "How long do I wait? How patient should I be?" Of course, the answer is "That depends." I would suggest you've waited long enough when you can confirm there is no life left in the idea, all avenues have been exhausted, and the opportunity cost is increasingly greater than the cost to wait. But, other than that, fight on, mighty warrior—wait for it!

5. Definition. While an idea may start out as a general thought or notion, you will need to get more specific before you put the pieces in place to fully develop your idea into a reality. You must put your idea on paper. This exercise will not only benefit you and the maturation of the idea but will benefit your team and potential clients as well. When your idea flows from your mind through your pencil onto paper, thoughts will disentangle themselves and start to become more orderly. One tip for helping you write your idea on paper is to imagine yourself telling your customer or client about the idea in a very conversational manner. How would you explain it? What will it do? What are its benefits? What are the risks? Why should anyone pay you money for this idea? What will it cost? As you go further and further down this road, your idea must have sufficient detail so that those around you understand your idea and all its implications, from early development all the way to market. It's not conceivable to think of every possible implication, but you

must try to think of as many as you can, adjusting your idea's details as you progress. It should be clear to every person on your team exactly what this idea is and how you plan to develop it.

6. Competencies. Once you figure out what your idea is and what it needs to get to market or to fully realize its potential, then you must consider what competencies or talents you will need to ensure success. For example, if my idea is a song, I first have to define it, which means I've written out the tune so a professional musician could read it. Based on the tune and how I wrote it, I know what instruments I'll need so it can be properly performed. I might need a piano, drums, bass, and guitar, as well as a saxophone. Those are the competencies I must ensure are available for my musical idea to succeed.

   It's the same with your business idea. Consider what your idea needs in the way of talent and skills, and make sure it is available. Putting a drummer in place and handing him saxophone music will not work. I must have the right match of talents and skills. So when you decide what competencies you need, then you must either get the training yourself, train someone on your team, bring on new employees with those competencies, or outsource what you need. Make sure you have the right people with the right skills.

7. Resources. One of the worst things that can happen to an entrepreneur and their idea is to run short of resources. If you've walked through this list of necessities above, by now you have a good idea of what you need. It's now time to get out your spreadsheets and start adding up the list of resources you will need to ensure your idea has a good chance to materialize. When we talk resources, we usually mean cash,

because most of the time that's what it all comes down to. But we might also find that we need office or warehouse space, vehicles or transportation services, information technology of some form or fashion, raw materials, machinery, and so on. This all depends on the idea, of course. The main point here is to make sure you have enough resources to get to market, to remain in the market long enough to give your idea plenty of time to succeed, and to weather any unforeseen circumstances that often arise.

Get together with your team, friends, or family and do some brainstorming about what might go wrong and what might go right. If things go wrong, consider how you might mitigate the damage or loss. If things go right, consider how you might handle the demand growth and properly support the customers after the sale. Once you've figured out what you need in terms of resources, give yourself another 25 percent buffer to account for anything else you haven't thought of yet. Where you get your resources is a diverse field, but most folks look to family, friends, their own savings or retirement accounts, or investors.

> *". . . be sure you have sufficient resources with some margin for the unexpected."*

Make sure you get legal advice when bringing on investors. A little due diligence up front could save you a tremendous amount of heartache and money later. Just remember the main message here: be sure you have sufficient resources with some margin for the unexpected.

8. Marketplace. Finally, a good idea needs a market. Whether your idea is an artistic or charitable one, or whether it's a business proposal, you need customers or users. Take the time

to define who your typical customer might be and get detailed about it. Consider where they are, what their income might be, and how they might pay for your idea. Target the most likely customers first. After you've experienced some success, you can always aim at another target group later. If you cannot readily define your target audience and where they might be located, do not proceed any further until you do.

This step is crucial. I know you'll be anxious to get things rolling, but you must consider your target customer. For example, if you've decided your target customer is located all over the country, perhaps using a retail website might be better than a storefront operation so you have access to more customers. Or if you decide your idea is best suited to a certain location, a storefront might make more sense. Take time to consider this aspect carefully. You might also consider testing the market you are targeting before fully committing to a location or business model.

You can achieve some success without everything in this list being just right, but I don't think you can achieve sustained success with the ability to survive debilitating onslaughts to your business without these needs being properly considered and managed.

Make sure your idea has what it needs to succeed.

PRINCIPLE 2

Your ideas are powerful. Make sure they have what they need to succeed.

CHAPTER THREE

Are You Thinking Right About the Problem?

"We can't solve problems by using the same kind of thinking we used when we created them."

—Albert Einstein

TWO BACKPACKERS, JIM AND Dale, were enjoying a lovely cool spring day in the mountains. The sun was shining, not a cloud in the sky, the birds were singing, and all was right with the world. Suddenly, a very large and apparently hungry grizzly bear came barreling out of the trees, headed straight for them. Realizing they were in great danger, they began running as fast they could, away from the bear. They soon realized the grizzly was gaining on them and gaining very fast. Running as fast as he could, Jim turned to see where Dale was and was shocked to see him sitting down, taking off his boots, and putting on his sneakers, which he'd just taken out of his backpack.

Jim yelled, "Dale, what are you doing? You're going to die if you sit there any longer. Run, man, run!" Dale calmly smiled and said, "Jim, you're not thinking about the problem right. You think the problem is a fierce grizzly bear and the solution is to run as fast as you can. But the *real* problem is who can run the fastest and what can be done to ensure the greatest foot speed possible. You see, I don't have outrun the bear. I only have to outrun you!"

Many of you have probably heard that joke before, or a form of it. But it clearly sets up the point I wish to make. Much of what we do to manage problems or challenges in business and life requires us to first properly assess our situation. Often the situation is fairly straightforward, not requiring our highest and best thinking. But sometimes things aren't so clear cut. The big risk is that if you don't clearly understand what is going on, you will *not* be able to come up with good, viable alternatives, and your course of action will most certainly be a huge mistake, costing you time, money, and who knows what else. I believe we often get ourselves into the worst situations when we aren't thinking right about our problems.

Some years ago, my firm was doing a logistic analysis of how a very large organization utilized a major seaport. The customer believed that they were not moving their material through this seaport quickly or efficiently enough, and it was costing them too much money and time. Before we got involved, they did several studies on their own, showing that it was taking nine to twelve days for material to move from its originating point through this port, and on to the customer. It's important to note that they were moving very large items, like vehicles, large trucks, and mountains of other stuff. In a twelve-day period, the value of the material they were moving was in the hundreds of millions of dollars. This was a huge challenge and cost driver. The longer these items took to get to their customers, the more their overhead went up and corresponding profits went down. Their market was very competitive with margins sometimes very thin. Other organizations were doing this better than them, which caused much frustration and irritation.

Frequently, the seaport was so jammed up that their incoming ships had to anchor off the coast and wait until a space came open on the pier. Having expensive assets like large cargo vessels just sitting off the coast, waiting on pier space, was very inefficient and costly.

This was also the only seaport available, so they had no choice but to use it. They were quite frustrated with it all. They tried adding more material-handling equipment, such as forklifts, cranes, and trucks. But they saw almost no difference in the process. They added more people, thinking maybe they were just shorthanded. Again, almost no change. They tried tweaking with the movement process and saw a small improvement, but not enough to matter. They were already working around the clock, so they couldn't find more capacity by working longer hours. There were only twenty-four hours in a day.

They turned to us for assistance. My young team of analysts didn't have as much experience as the customer with this seaport, but they were also unconstrained in their thinking and were able to view the question with fresh eyes. This was key. First my team drew a flowchart model of the current process to fully understand what was happening. They then turned the flowchart into a computer simulation. Next they began the process of "playing tunes" with the simulation—that is, inserting or deleting capability at each step of the process. They were looking for the most sensitive point in the process. They were attempting to make sure they understood the problem properly—or make sure they were thinking right about the problem, much like Dale in the bear story mentioned earlier.

We did find the problem. It turns out the pier infrastructure wasn't configured optimally for the kind of ships this customer was using. Ships offload their material differently, depending on how they're built. These ships didn't match the pier structure very well. We found that for an investment of $1.5 million, the customer could reconfigure the pier and reduce the process from twelve days to six days or less. The experienced employees in the customer's company didn't even think about changing the pier structure. In the past, the issues were always resolved with more trucks, forklifts, cranes, and people. They were constrained by their own experience. *They were thinking incorrectly about the problem.* If you had asked them, "Is this pier configured properly?" they might have discovered the same problem we did. But that wasn't what they were thinking.

When the customer saw our analysis and verified it, they were extremely happy and quite willing to spend the $1.5 million. Compared to the value of goods going through that port and the time saved, it was an investment that would quickly pay for itself. It was an "Aha" moment for them.

Questions to Ask Yourself

It would be impossible to magically see each and every problem you face correctly. We're all human and prone to mistakes, biases, and constrained thinking. No one can know and see it all. But there are some things you can do to increase your chances of right thinking.

Below are my suggestions for helping you see the problem correctly:

1. First, accept that you don't know it all. I know this sounds obvious, but I'm speaking from my own experience. One of the biggest constraints in my thinking was often me. I would think, "I've got this," when in fact I didn't. Be honest with yourself. Consider for a moment that you might not understand what is actually happening. Talk to a trusted friend or colleague who cares about you and your business. Examine every assumption. Ask yourself, "What am I missing? What have I overlooked?" Make sure you are seeing clearly, and understand what you are looking at.

2. Listen, listen, listen. One of your greatest skills as a business owner or entrepreneur is your ability to listen—really listen. Often your client, spouse, or partner is telling you what the problem is, but you have to be a good listener to get it. They don't always know what the real problem or question is, but they try to communicate it as best they can. You have to try to listen and "read between the lines." One good question to

ask yourself, as you are listening to them, is, "Am I listening to respond or to understand?" Or put another way, when someone is talking to you, are you forming your answer while they are speaking, or are you focused only on understanding what you're hearing? One good way to ensure you are listening to understand is to repeat back to them what they just said, from *their perspective.* For example, after hearing a comment or question, you could say, "Okay, so just to check my understanding, what I think I heard you say was . . ." and then repeat what they said *as they would describe it.*

3. What is the question being asked? Make sure you've identified the right question and understand all its attributes and implications. When someone asks which alternative is best, you should ask, "What do you mean by best? Fastest, cheapest, quickest, lightest?" etc. *If you don't identify the right question, you will answer the wrong one.* Take the time you need to validate you have the right question. This will usually take some work. You might find yourself on a trip of discovery, not knowing what you'll find until you find it. Like our bear joke earlier, the critical idea was *not* to outrun the bear, but to outrun the other person.

4. What are the scope and boundaries of the problem? Often just by accurately defining the boundaries of the problem, you completely eliminate some of the outlying alternatives, making your choices fewer and simpler. No analytics needed here, just common sense. In my seaport example above, we weren't trying to solve the customer's global logistic problems, just the issues at one seaport. As it turns out, the solution we offered for the seaport led to other solutions for this customer at other seaports, and that's great. But we didn't start out trying to solve a global issue. Set the scope and boundaries and maintain them.

5. What assumptions are you making? Most of the time, your assumptions make or break your understanding of the problem, as it did in the story about Jim and Dale. Make sure you know your assumptions. For example, if someone has indeed asked which answer is "best," challenge your assumptions on what defines "best." I've often found that what I always thought was "best" really wasn't. Keep "peeling the onion" back, layer by layer, and you'll eventually get to the real question that you need to understand and answer. And, usually, when your client or partner hears the real or better question, they'll know it immediately. Again, you will most likely find yourself on a trip of discovery.

Stop Talking and Just Listen

My wife and I were discussing a problem once. As was often my habit, I was listening to her to try to find out what I needed to do to solve the problem. As she spoke, I was forming potential solutions, thinking of how long it would take to solve, how much it might cost, so I'd be ready to present my solution when she finished telling me her concerns about the problem. I tried at several intervals during our discussion to lay out my solution, but I could tell she was not feeling any better about it all. So I kept tossing out additional ideas, and she appeared to grow even more frustrated.

Finally, she said, "Stop trying to solve the problem. I don't want you to solve it. I just want you to listen to me." I was shocked. She didn't want me to solve the problem? Really?

Over time, I slowly began to realize that my loving wife wanted connection and conversation more than she wanted me to try to solve all our problems. I wasn't thinking correctly about the situation, going about it the wrong way, and was trying to solve the wrong problem. I was missing the point completely. Once I finally understood and learned to just listen, these conversations went much better, often ending with no resolution, which was hard for me to just accept sometimes, but she was much happier. I had to learn that I was addressing the wrong problem; I wasn't thinking right. I was answering the wrong question or approaching the problem the wrong way.

The last thing I'll offer on this topic of thinking correctly is a three-step process I sometimes use to make sure I get started right:

1. Do what you have to do to make sure you have a clear view of the issue or question. Understand the scope and boundaries. Make sure you aren't missing any parts of it. Get it all in front of you. If you were looking at a team sport and only looked at the offensive side of the game, you'd not be considering the whole game properly. You must also consider the defensive side of the game. Make sure you see it all.

2. Now that you see it all clearly, do you understand what you're looking at? Do more research, talk to more experts, whiteboard your thoughts, draw out the process, or question to further explore all of its implications, dimensions, and relationships.

3. Content that you see and understand the question now, use your wisdom and experience to now set up an approach to resolve it.

Getting your mind properly set is critical to problem-solving.

PRINCIPLE 3

Make sure you understand the question or problem and are thinking correctly about it. If you don't identify the right question, you will answer the wrong one.

CHAPTER FOUR

What Do You Believe About Yourself?

"You become what you believe, not what you think or what you want."

—Oprah Winfrey

FOR NINE YEARS, THE record time for running one mile hovered just above four minutes. As early as 1945, Gunder Haegg had approached the barrier with a time of 4:01.4. Many people said the four-minute barrier would never be broken. It simply defied man's physical limits. But in 1954, Roger Bannister broke the tape at 3:59.4. And what was the result? Well, as soon as the myth of the "impossible barrier" was dispelled, many world-class milers bettered the four-minute mark. In almost no time, the four-minute achievement was broken sixty-six times by twenty-six different runners!

What can we learn from this true story? To me, it's about the power of our personal belief system, the power to positively *and* negatively impact our lives, our performance, our businesses, even our dreams. You've heard it said, "If you believe you can, or you believe you can't, you are right!" Roger Bannister obviously believed he could break the four-minute mile. But after he did it, many others quickly followed. Why? Because after Roger did it, their faith grew and they believed they could do it, too.

If you simply dismiss this notion as hopeful thinking or naivete, I think you miss the larger point. Almost any world-class athlete will tell you that believing in yourself is critical to success. I've heard some say that they "see themselves" winning. By this I think they mean they use their powers of imagination and picture themselves crossing the finish line first, which increases their faith in themselves, and they begin to believe they will make it happen.

I've heard professional golfers tell me when they are preparing to hit the next shot, standing over the ball and looking at the fairway ahead, they decide where they want to ball to go. They then imagine the ball's flight and how they will hit it. They see the shot first before they hit it. They believe if they execute the shot as imagined, a good outcome will result. Of course, not every shot goes where they hope, but they do it right often enough to make them want to continue this habit.

Or perhaps you've seen a winter Olympic athlete in the downhill skiing competition. Moments before they start down the hill, you will see them, with eyes closed, imagining themselves skiing down the hill. They sway left, then right, pretending to jump and move as if they're already moving down the hill. They are imagining the run before they do it. They believe if they know and execute their plan well, they will succeed—and they often do.

I think our ability to see the future with our mind's eye, to picture something before it happens, to use our imaginations to explore alternatives and corresponding outcomes, is one of the things that makes us different from every other living thing on this planet. Our imaginations can be extremely powerful, both for good and bad. We can imagine good things happening and be encouraged, or we can imagine bad things happening and become fearful. We love to be encouraged, but we don't like to fear.

Fear can be a good thing. As a protective mechanism, it can help us stay out of harm's way. But when it is allowed to consume our thinking where we fearfully obsess over an outcome, it can be a real detriment to us, causing us to make poor decisions, even negatively affecting our health. Finding that healthy balance is key. It is one thing to consider an outcome with all its good and bad alternatives, and it is quite another to fearfully obsess over it.

"It is one thing to consider an outcome with all its good and bad alternatives, and it is quite another to fearfully obsess over it."

Let's look a little closer at this notion that your beliefs can affect outcomes in your business and life.

What Ultimately Drives Outcomes?

Figure 2.

I think your beliefs drive your decisions, and your decisions determine your outcomes. But it all starts with your beliefs. I first heard Pastor Andy Stanley of Atlanta, Georgia, discuss this concept. See Figure 2 above. Where we often make our mistake is when our outcomes don't materialize as we'd hoped, we go back to the decision we made, examine it, adjust, and make another decision. Unfortunately, we often find the outcome once again is not the one we wanted. With the figure above in mind, what we should do when we don't get the right outcome is to go all the way back to the left, beyond our decision, and examine our beliefs.

For example, let's look at a fictitious situation where you've been turned down when you asked someone special out on a date. Let's say you asked them to go with you to a chamber music recital. They were kind but declined, saying they had other commitments. So, doing what most people do, again keeping the above figure in mind, you go back to the decision you made and make another. You ask them out again to a fancy restaurant. Again, they tell you they're busy and regretfully say no. You continue to do this, again and again with the same outcome. Finally, you remember what you read in this book about the belief-decision-outcome cycle and decide to go all the way back and examine your beliefs about this situation.

Your first belief is (1) this person doesn't generally object to going out with me (2) if I find the right situation, and (3) if they are available, they will go out with me. You also believe that (4) you're an attractive person, (5) people generally like you, want to be around you, and (6) given the option would go out with you when asked. But after being turned down so many times, you decide you must look critically at your beliefs.

You seek the counsel of an honest friend and tell them all about your situation and your beliefs and decisions and outcomes. Your friend, who is indeed a true friend, tells you that your beliefs are not quite right. You learn that your intended date is extremely shy and will only go out with people the first time if they are in a group setting, never alone. You learn your intended date has been the victim of horrible relationship experiences previously, explaining why they are so hesitant to date.

With this new information, you adjust your beliefs. Your new beliefs lead you to make a new decision for a group get-together with friends, including your intended date. You make it friendly, fun, and low-key. You invite your hopeful date again. This time they accept. Eureka! This could be the start of something very special.

> ***"Our beliefs must be sound for our decisions to have any hope of success."***

If you think about your own situation, perhaps you've been frustrated repeatedly with unintended or undesired outcomes. Have you only been looking at your decisions and trying to adjust those? You're like most people, me included. If your building is built upon a poor foundation, the walls will crack, the floor will not be level, and nothing you do to the building's walls or aboveground structure will fix the problem. The foundation must be set on good footings, or all else will be futile. It's the same with our beliefs. They must be sound for our decisions to have any hope of success.

What do you tell yourself? What do you believe about your situation? What do you imagine you can do? Can you picture yourself winning? Succeeding? Failing? Can you imagine what that would look like?

We all have the ability to believe, to imagine, to have faith and hope. As mentioned before, if you know, understand, and experience fear, then you already have the ability to know, understand, and experience faith. It's like a muscle, but if you don't exercise it, you lose it. And, like a muscle, the more you use it, the stronger it gets.

I hope what I just said excites and encourages you. You have the ability already built within to believe in yourself and change your outcomes.

> ***"You have the ability already built within to believe in yourself and change your outcomes."***

So, how do we use this ability for good in our lives and for those people and causes we care about? How do you stop the harmful negative beliefs and turn them to the positive? Below are some suggestions evolved from my own experience.

1. Surround yourself with encouraging people who care about you. This is perhaps the easiest and best way to start changing your beliefs. The more we hear encouragement, the more we are encouraged. Of course, the opposite is also true, which is why we have to put ourselves in the proper situation with the right people. We are better versions of ourselves when we live in a community that cares about us and that we care about.

2. Study those who have succeeded in their chosen field, be it athletics, business, research, art, etc. What were their stories? Try to find out what they believed about themselves. For example, in the case of Roger Bannister above, no one had run the four-minute mile before he did. I'm sure he believed he could break the barrier as he approached that race. And after he did it, it was easier for others to believe they could do it. Study people like Roger.

3. Imagine what success would look like to you. See it with your mind's eye. Write that down in your journal. Ask yourself what would need to happen for your dreams to become reality. Write that down. Discuss this with your family or community. I'm guessing they will encourage you, advise you, and cheer you on. You need this.

4. Set near-term, intermediate, and long-term goals for yourself to accomplish what you wrote down from the previous paragraph. Make your goals achievable and actionable. Be specific about milestones you wish to reach and when you'd like to accomplish them. Celebrate when you reach a milestone, and make adjustments when you don't. Most of all, give yourself permission to fail without guilt or fear. Tell yourself you're either winning or learning, but never losing.

The more you accomplish, the more your beliefs will grow. But for those times when success seems out of reach and your discouragement grows, use your support system: your community—those encouraging people you've surrounded yourself with.

Any gardener knows that if you properly care for your plants, they will produce for you. You must treat your beliefs the same way, feeding and caring for them properly as I've suggested above. In this way, your ability to believe in yourself will grow. I also think you'll find that knowledge and experience will dispel fear. The more you know, and the more experienced you become at having faith in yourself, the less fear will influence your mind and decision-making. Strengthen that muscle of belief.

PRINCIPLE 4

What you believe about yourself and your situation will drive your decisions, and your decisions determine your outcomes. Change your beliefs to change your decisions and thereby your outcomes.

CHAPTER FIVE

Finding Your Purpose and Direction

"The two most important days in your life are the day you were born, and the day you find out why."

—Mark Twain

NO MATTER YOUR RACE or religion, social or economic status, every person on this earth has several things in common with his fellow man. I'm not talking about the basic physical needs of food, clothing, or shelter, even though those are common to us all. And I'm not thinking about our need for loving relationships, to be in community with others, and to worship someone or something. I'm thinking of something else, beyond just the relational and spiritual needs we share.

Each and every one of us has a deep-seated desire to live a life of purpose, a life of meaning, a life that justifies our existence. We cannot stand the thought of our lives being wasted or lived for no reason. We all want our family and friends to be able to easily say that the world is a better place because we were in it.

This need for purpose extends outward and touches all that we do. We want our chosen professions to be purposeful and not just about making a living. We want our personal relationships to be a part of our purpose, believing they are woven into and benefiting our grand plan in life. We want to be part of something bigger than ourselves, something of benefit to mankind, if not globally, then at least in our own neighborhoods.

As parents, we want our children to grow up with purpose, to live worthy of the opportunities we hope to provide them, to live for bigger causes than just pleasing themselves or satisfying their material desires.

"We cannot stand the thought of our lives being wasted."

So, given that purpose is so critical to us all, it then follows that there are two important days to note in our lives, as Mark Twain said: the day we are born, and the day we know why. I'm not saying these are necessarily the most important days of our lives, but they are nonetheless very important to us, personally. Of course, the day we were born is important because that started it all! Everything in life has to have a beginning.

It's the second day that can sometimes be more elusive—the day we finally realize why we were born. For those of you who have already experienced that second day, who know why you were born, who have a strong sense of your purpose, well done! It's safe to say your life has undoubtedly been more meaningful since that day. Hopefully, you've been enjoying fulfilling your purpose, and those around you have benefited from your efforts.

Those that haven't yet experienced that second day are probably asking, "What is my purpose? How do I discover it?" You sincerely want to know but have been frustrated in your attempts to find it. How can anyone know their true purpose in life? There are as many answers to this question as there are people asking it. But I have some thoughts that could help you find your purpose.

Thoughts on Finding Your Purpose

1. Be honest with yourself. This is the first and most obvious piece of advice I can give. Often you really do know your purpose, or at least have a strong indication of what it is, but don't want to believe or accept it. Possibly the thought of it scares you since it seems so impossible. You don't feel qualified or worthy, so your self-talk shuts you down, and with it, your purpose. Please be honest and share your true feelings with someone who cares about you. Listen to their feedback. Don't limit yourself in finding your true purpose out of fear or unbelief. Give yourself permission to dream. If you're not honest with yourself, you might be depriving others of the benefit of your true gift and depriving yourself of your true purpose and the happiness and sense of fulfillment that goes with it.

2. Consider: what do people most often ask of you? Are you the person everyone comes to see when they want advice on their finances, on their professional goals, on raising their children, on relationships, or even on car repairs? Often the thing that everyone comes to you for is a strong indicator concerning your purpose. I believe we are all gifted in some way where we excel at one or more things above others. Our gifts will usually complement our purpose. Discover your gifts and you may find your purpose.

3. Consider: what things come easily for you? Similar to the paragraph above, what sorts of things come easily for you that seem to be harder for others? That also can be evidence that will lead to the discovery of your purpose. To illustrate, if you are good with numbers, you might find that your future will involve quantitative jobs: accountant, stockbroker, financial manager, personal financial planner, statistician, and so on. Then you might find that you are always being asked to help others balance their checkbooks or set up a budget. Your

purpose could be as a personal financial planner, helping others get out and stay out of financial trouble. What a great purpose!

4. Consider: what brings you joy? Finally, the things that you love to do that give you great satisfaction are another strong piece of evidence that could lead you to your purpose. You might love to teach people things that improve their lives, while others would find this boring and unpleasant. You might find fulfillment using your skills in charitable work. You might enjoy playing a musical instrument. I once met a guitarist. Nothing unusual about that. But it's where I met him that was unique.

   I was in a hospital ICU, visiting my father, and I met him in the next room. I'd heard his acoustic guitar and was curious to see what was going on. I listened for a moment. He was quite good. His acoustic guitar had a lovely tone, and he was very skilled. I pulled him aside and asked why he was here. He said the hospital was trying a new program to bring music to patients who were working to heal or overcome great illness or injury. It was an experimental program but had shown great promise with the patients by bringing joy and the contentment that music can bring, improving their mental health. As a volunteer, this initiative brought him great joy, and he was very committed to the program. What a wonderful purpose!

5. Consider: what doors are open to you now? Sometimes, you may find that you are blessed to have an unexpected opportunity staring you in the face—an opportunity that comes only once in a great while. You had nothing to do with it. The conditions just materialized out of thin air, but it's a great opportunity. Yes, there are other things that you might have been thinking about doing or even actively pursuing, but this serendipitous opportunity looks good and you think

> you might enjoy it. Don't let perfect be the enemy of the good. Consider taking the opportunity. Often an unexpected open door is the most obvious indicator of your calling or purpose. If it doesn't work out, you can always change course.

It may take some time to discover your purpose, but it's worth the effort. Don't get anxious about it. Take it a day at a time, in a steady fashion. It will come. You will know it when you see it. Your patience will be rewarded. Don't force the process of discovery, either. There's few situations in life I can think of where forcing the issue is a good thing. Giving yourself time to find your purpose is critical.

Regarding my own journey, I wasn't honest with myself. I clearly saw evidence of my gifts and talents, things I easily excelled in. But I did not want to go where they led. I had fears and misgivings about them. I wanted something else—I thought. One day, a good and trusted friend persuaded me to explore the purpose I was avoiding. "What have you got to lose?" he asked. So I went with my gifts. It changed my life for the better. My fears and misgivings were unfounded. I now feel I have a good sense of my purpose, and I'm so much happier than when I was avoiding it and not being honest with myself.

• • •

Having a purpose gives our lives context, meaning, and hope. It helps us set a course for our lives. When needed, it can also help us change course. After our purpose is known, it doesn't usually sit still, never changing. Things change. Desires change. As we gain knowledge and experience, our purpose can evolve. This will often lead to the need to change our course to continue our purpose.

As things change in our lives, as our desires change or evolve and we see the need for a course correction, how do we do that? You might say, "Hey, once I set my direction in life, I don't intend ever to change. Consistency is key, right?" I do agree consistency is good, but adaptability may be even more important. The ability to adapt in business is critical for survival. For example, let's say we're back in the 1970s. Your purpose is to provide the very latest 8-track audio cassette playing experience possible for every automobile on the market. (I'm dating myself, I know.) You offer people the best speakers, 8-track cassette players, and quality installation. What happens when the market moves to the smaller cassette players, as we now know it did? What about when the market moves to compact disc players? What happens when the market moves to digital music on digital devices? If you haven't changed course, your business is dead.

It's no different when we're talking about our life's purpose and direction. We have to always keep our minds open to course corrections. The "set it and forget it" mindset can be very costly and damaging in this context. Most of your course changes will be small, incremental ones; very few will be major. But consider in a rocket going to the moon, if you were off by one degree in your course, you'd miss the moon by 4,169 miles (nearly twice the diameter of the moon[7]). So, while most course changes in your life and business may be small, they nonetheless have a major influence on your outcomes.

It May Be Time to Change Course

I am a sailor. For twelve years, I owned a forty-nine-foot sailing yacht. Once, while sailing with friends on my planned course, the weather and wind changed dramatically, and I found I was having a horrible time holding my course. I also found that my passengers were not happy since this course was at the very least making them uncomfortable due to the extreme motions of the boat and at the most making them seasick. Our lovely outing was turning into a regrettable experience. If you've ever been seasick, then you know how completely it can ruin your day. Something had to change.

7 A Mere One Degree of Difference by Antone Roundy (https://whitehat-crew.com/blog/a-mere-one-degree-difference/)

One of the things you learn as a sailor is to take what the weather gives you—don't stubbornly stick to your course when there's a better alternative. Yes, you must start out with a plan, but you must be ready and willing to change, both for the comfort and safety of all on board and the material condition of the vessel. If there's an alternative course or approach that will get you to your destination and help your passengers enjoy the experience more and prevent damage to your boat, then you must take it. If you stubbornly hold your course, you may be sailing alone next time, and that's no fun. Sailing with friends is what it's all about.

Again, taking what the weather gave me, I changed our destination and course. Rather than going to point A, which had a lovely restaurant, I chose to go to point B, which also had a lovely restaurant. The motion of the boat changed immediately to something much more palatable, and the day was not only saved but everyone had a great time. Had I held my original course, I believe we most certainly would have arrived, but no one would have felt like eating. So the wonderful restaurant at point A would have been a moot point, to say nothing of my popularity with my guests.

Charting a New Course in Business and Life

If you one day realize that the course you are on, whether in business or life, is not working, you must consider changing your course or direction. To keep the same course could be detrimental to your people and your business. Someone once said, "Insanity is doing the same thing over and over again and expecting different results."[8] I know changing course can be scary. You've planned and set your heart on a certain direction. You know the current course well. You've put a lot into it emotionally, mentally, and physically. But don't let the specter of change keep you from making a critical change in direction. Take a moment, step back, and examine the question carefully.

---

8 This quote is usually attributed to Albert Einstein, but there is some disagreement as to who might have first said it.

Here are my tips when you believe a course change may be needed.

1. Gain new perspective. You first need to change how you see things. As a sailor, I needed to go to my charts and see the bigger picture: what navigational hazards are around me, how much room I have, what the clouds and weather are indicating, how much time I have before it gets too dark. You can see the similarities between my sailing example and what you must do for your situation. All these things will give you a better picture you may not be seeing currently. Also, put yourself in the place of all stakeholders and ask, "How might they see things?" In fact, if you feel you can safely do this without hindering your efforts, ask your stakeholders how they see your situation.

2. Understand the problem. Now that you've broadened your perspective and are hopefully seeing things more comprehensively, take the time to make sure you understand what you're looking at—that you know the real problem. For example, remember the joke about the two hikers running from a hungry grizzly bear. The one who suddenly stops and begins putting on sneakers insists, "You don't understand the problem. I only have to outrun you, not the bear." Make sure you understand the real problem. It may not be obvious. Another set of eyes and ears would be very helpful at this point. Ask someone you trust and who cares about you sincerely to take a look at the question. Their honest feedback can be most valuable.

3. Find the opportunity. With every problem comes an opportunity. Look for the vulnerability, the gap or deficiency. What would solve the problem? How well situated are you to respond to it? What would it take to be in a good position to respond? What would it cost? How long would it take

to develop this capability? What are the risks? These and other questions should be asked to properly understand the opportunity.

4. Develop your plan. Get your best and brightest talent together and build your plan. Cost it out. Wargame it (test it). Identify the risks and the corresponding mitigation strategies. Weigh the alternatives.

5. Commit and change course. If you decide on a specific course change, don't flip-flop back and forth. Until some obvious condition changes the situation, making it no longer a good course, you and your people must commit and chart this new course. Make sure you give your new course time to produce the desired results. Don't abandon it too quickly. By the same token, don't ride it all the way to the bottom, either.

Be Prepared to Adjust Your Course

Rarely will you ever make a single course change and "set it and forget it." You will most likely have to make frequent small corrections to stay on course. And you may have to go back to the first step in the list above and start again if the conditions change drastically. But with a watchful eye, an open mind, and a solid team alongside you, you'll weather the business and life storms well.

PRINCIPLE 5

If you haven't already found your purpose, begin an unforced journey of discovery. Allow your purpose to emerge in an honest way. Then let your purpose set your course in life. Be willing to change course as conditions change.

CHAPTER SIX

What You Allow to Influence Your Major Decisions

"Sometimes you make the right decision, and sometimes you make the decision right."

—Phil McGraw

WHEN YOU ARE FACED with making a major decision, you must ensure that you give it the time and care it deserves. You must stay focused on your purpose to ensure that you do not allow things that have no real bearing or positive impact on your goal to influence your decision.

Several years ago, I was faced with a major business decision, one that would have a significant effect on my employees and our financial health. I was already extremely busy with several business development efforts, and I had some significant personal issues going on in my life at the time. This decision was a difficult one, both in terms of complexity and execution. Done correctly, it would require a lot of my time and attention to get it right.

Because of other influencing factors, which had nothing to do with the decision, I took some shortcuts, hoping to get to an answer quicker. I also allowed my other worries, unrelated to the decision, to influence me toward a particular outcome. Every time I sat down to study the decision, I was either too tired or completely distracted by other pressing issues to do a good job. Of the many alternatives I had to choose from, I was very tempted just to make a choice and move on. I reasoned that if it turned out wrong, I could adjust later or cancel and start over. I was completely wrong. It was only the quick thinking of one of my employees that prevented me from making an expensive and morale-busting decision. They encouraged me to allow myself more time.

When I finally did stop and take the time to understand it all, allowing no other undue or unrelated things to influence me, I made the right decision. It saved us a lot of money and was a big hit with the employees.

"Let your goals and purpose influence your decisions."

The lesson here is to let your goals and purpose influence your decisions, not your worries, challenges, fears, setbacks, disgruntled employees, or problems at home. Focus on the purpose and goals you are trying to achieve and avoid the negative or improper influences that can sometimes occur and get you heading the wrong direction.

For me, when my employee helped me see I was about to make an error, I slowed down. Often that is the best solution. If you can't give your major decision the time and care it needs and avoid undue influence from anything except your goals, then it's best to delay it. It's better to take longer and get the decision right than hurry, getting it wrong and having to do damage control.

Another reason to take the proper amount of time for your decision is to make sure you understand what's going on. I served twenty years in the US Navy. When I was aboard ship, we would often run fire drills to make sure we were ready to respond to this very dangerous scenario. What most people don't realize about sailors and war is that when they die, they usually die trying to save themselves and their shipmates from a fire or flooding within the ship. We usually think of soldiers or Marines dying on the field of battle; not so with sailors. We take fires and flooding very seriously.

One thing I learned in basic naval officer training about fighting fires and flooding is that the first reports of a casualty are *almost always wrong.* This isn't opinion. Massive amounts of casualty data collected over many decades have confirmed this, again and again. If you're the officer on the bridge responsible for operating the ship and you get a frantic report of fire from somewhere within the ship, it's almost always incorrect. Even though there may be something horrible happening, you must take the time to be certain you understand the situation before you begin issuing orders to the crew.

If you acted on the first report by taking a drastic step regarding the power plant or dispatched an emergency response team to the reported location, you could actually make things much worse and slow the recovery from the emergency. This could easily cause further damage to the ship and, more importantly, cost the precious lives of the crew. We were taught to take a minute to get confirmation of a first report—a second set of eyes, a reading of an instrument, a measurement, anything to independently confirm the situation. When you have the confirmation, you can then more confidently take actions to recover from the casualty. This was our training.

Once, when I was at sea on the bridge, we got a frantic call from somewhere within the ship reporting a fire. This was not a drill. The sailor reported the fire, where it was, and what kind it was (electrical, fuel, or something else). Our captain was on the bridge at the time. He was often out touring the ship, checking the condition of the ship and crew. But not this time. He very calmly grabbed the microphone, announced the emergency to the entire crew so general preparations could begin to ready our response to the fire, then asked a work station that was near the reported location of the fire to check the report. Within thirty seconds, he had a second report from a different and more experienced member of the crew. The second report confirmed it was a fire, indeed. The location was close enough, but the type of fire reported was wrong. Had the captain dispatched a fire response team ready to fight a fuel fire, as reported, there would have been delays as the team would have been readying to address the wrong kind of fire. It was an electrical fire, which requires a very different response than a fuel fire.

The good news is the fire was caught very early and wasn't a problem at all, even with the incorrect first report. The most important action was the timeliness of the report. But the second most important was an accurate report. By taking one more minute to confirm the real situation, the correct response was made and the fire put out quickly.

My point is this: if the Navy can take just an extra moment to confirm things before making decisions in a life-or-death crisis, we can most certainly take extra time to confirm our own business or life situations before we make a decision committing talent and treasure to a major decision. You have the time. Make sure you clearly understand what's going on before taking action.

PRINCIPLE 6

Let your goals and purpose influence your major decisions, not your worries, challenges, fears, setbacks, disgruntled employees, or problems at home. And take the time the decision deserves.

Part One Recap: How Do You Think?

PRINCIPLE 1

Your business and life are interdependent, one affecting the other, and must be kept in balance.

PRINCIPLE 2

Your ideas are powerful. Make sure they have what they need to succeed.

PRINCIPLE 3

Make sure you understand the question or problem and are thinking correctly about it. If you don't identify the right question, you will answer the wrong one.

PRINCIPLE 4

What you believe about yourself and your situation will drive your decisions, and your decisions determine your outcomes. Change your beliefs to change your decisions and thereby your outcomes.

PRINCIPLE 5

If you haven't already found your purpose, begin an unforced journey of discovery. Allow your purpose to emerge in an honest way. Then let your purpose set your course in life. Be willing to change course as conditions change.

PRINCIPLE 6

Let your goals and purpose influence your major decisions, not your worries, challenges, fears, setbacks, disgruntled employees, or problems at home. And take the time the decision deserves.

PART TWO:

THE TOP THINGS I WISH I'D KNOWN BEFORE STARTING MY BUSINESS

CHAPTER SEVEN

Three Keys to Keep Your Life and Business in Balance

"When a force acts to put you out of balance, an opposite and equal force must be applied to compensate."

AS ENTREPRENEURS, WE OFTEN have no problem getting motivated. After all, we are pursuing a dream—our own idea. We are inherently motivated. When I worked for someone else, I was not always excited to get up early every day and get to work. But when I started working for me, for my own dream, I was up very early and happy about it, eager to get to work. Nothing is more motivating that pursuing your own idea.

However, when we allow ourselves to get out of balance, problems arise. When we focus on nothing else but pursuing the dream, leaving all else aside, we do serious harm to ourselves and those we love and care deeply about. Our personal lives will suffer, our health will suffer, and our relationships will suffer. We become self-defeating even though we are pursuing something with great sincerity and honest devotion. Our ambition outstrips our noble intentions.

"Our ambition outstrips our noble intentions."

It is extremely critical that we maintain a balance between our personal and business lives. Why? Simply put, so that things can work properly—both in life and business. If you ride a bicycle, you know that the bicycle only works when things stay in balance. All the forces acting upon you and the bike have to be working in harmony to keep the thing upright and moving forward. How about an aircraft? If all the forces acting upon on it are not in balance, terrible things will result. My point is the same for you and the pursuit of your dream; it all has to stay in balance with the rest of your life, or it will not work. It will be unsustainable. You may get away with a short-term imbalance, but you most certainly will not over the longer term.

Where balance can really be helpful is when the storms of life and business come, and come they will. It's one thing to sustain a healthy business in good times. It's quite another to sustain it through the bad times (recall my own story in the introduction). Without question, a balanced condition will weather storms better than an imbalanced one.

Consider a sailboat. If too much sail is set and stormy winds come, the boat will be in great danger, out of balance, uncontrollably whipped about at the mercy of the stormy winds, and in danger of capsizing or broaching. When the high winds come, you must reduce the amount of sail to reduce the influence the wind has on the boat, keeping the amount of sail *in balance* with the amount of wind. If your sails are set properly, you can handle stormy winds. Yes, it might still be bumpy and uncomfortable, but you can carry on quite well until the more gentle breezes return. But if you're already out of balance and your sails are not set properly, an unexpected stormy gust of wind can be catastrophic. Keeping the boat properly balanced and configured gives you the best chance of handling any adverse conditions that may arise.

How Do You Know When You're Getting Out of Balance?

Sometimes it's easy to tell when you're out of balance. Sometimes it is not. Do you know what condition you are in? Is your situation in balance? An honest assessment is needed to confirm your situation. Below are some questions I suggest you ask yourself. This isn't meant to be an all-inclusive or scientific evaluation—it's only a guide to get you thinking. Be very honest with yourself and ask these questions:

1. Are there growing tensions between you and those closest to you—your spouse, or your friends? Do you seem to have more arguments? Is your communication with them poor and getting worse? Does conversation about the pursuit of your dream always end up in an argument or disagreement? Do you feel distance and space increasing between you and them? Do you find yourself snapping at those you love, getting angry quickly? Are you patient?

2. Are important dates always sneaking up on you, or do they go by without you noticing, such as anniversaries, birthdays, graduations, and other significant personal milestones for those that love you? Does it feel like you are always scrambling to keep up? Do you sometimes miss them completely? Has this negatively impacted your relationships?

3. Is your health suffering? Are you sleeping well? How are your eating habits? Do you consistently exercise? Are you often feeling like you're in a fog? Are details being missed? Maybe you're having more headaches? Are you gaining weight?

4. Are you taking time for yourself? Are you taking time for those you love? Are you reading good books, going to the theater or museum, or dining out with your favorite people? Are you having fun? When was the last time you had fun? Can you honestly say you experience joy on a regular basis?

5. Are you spending more money than you actually have? Financial health is a very good indicator of imbalance. Do you often find you have more month left than money? I have another chapter on spending. Make sure you read it and evaluate your actions against it.

6. Do you ever think about *anything* else besides your business or dream? Do you talk about sports news with friends? Do you discuss other hobbies or things you love to do with those around you? Are you one dimensional, seeming to always discuss the same thing over and over—your business or dream?

> ***"You must make the decision NOW to intentionally put your life in balance."***

Does any of that ring true with you? Does it hit close to home at all? Be honest. You might say, "Yes, that's all happening, but it's only temporary. When my business or dream gets on track, I'll get back on track, rebalance myself, and all will be well." Really? Are you sure? My experience has shown this will not be the case. There will always be something else that needs your time and attention. You will never "get on track." It never stops, believe me. You must make the decision NOW to intentionally put your life in balance and keep it that way.

How Do You Put Your Life in Balance?

Each person and situation is different, but there are some common steps that will apply to almost everyone to help you put your life back into balance or at least get you started in the right direction. As you read, think about the scale pictured below. When you place something on one of the plates, it will drop, and the other plate will rise. To balance the scale, you must put something of equal weight on the other plate to compensate. So, with that in mind, here are three key suggestions to help you get back to a state of balance.

Figure 3: A balanced scale.

Suggestion 1: Compensate. If your business or dream takes an unhealthy amount of time, you must compensate. Just like with the scale, you must put something on the other plate to balance it. For example, if your business caused you to work sixty or eighty hours this week, then carve out some hours next week for pleasure. You must schedule this time, or it probably won't happen. There is a set amount of time each week to live your life. It does not change. You cannot increase it. You must use it wisely. Within that time, you must allocate hours for work, family, and rest. When you exceed the allocated time in one area, you must compensate for it later in another area. This keeps the scale in balance. Yes, you can be imbalanced in the short term and survive, but my point is that living in an imbalanced state is not sustainable in the longer term.

Suggestion 2: Set Boundaries. Set boundaries for yourself as it relates to your business. Don't put yourself in a position where you are always reacting to whatever randomly happens every day. Set aside time in your day and week for business-related or work activity, personal time for thinking, planning, and journaling, and time for family and friends. After you set those boundaries, then *keep them*! If you always exceed them, they are useless. Don't let others cross those boundaries, either. If people know what you expect, they will respect it and assist you. You will also set a good example for those around you to keep their lives in balance.

Suggestion 3: Take Care. Don't forget to feed your mind, body, and soul. Read good books. See a collection at an art gallery. Attend a concert or the theater. Maintain a healthy diet and habit of exercise. Do acts of kindness and charity for others. Don't make your life all about yourself and your dreams, because it isn't. As a business owner or entrepreneur, your creative juices will cease to flow when your emotional or mental fuel tanks are empty. If you are always giving, giving, giving but never taking time to receive, you will run out of fuel, creatively and otherwise. Your life is a marathon, not a sprint. If you ran a marathon like a sprint, you'd lose quickly and every time. Pace yourself and take time to smell the roses along the way. It's the journey that's important, much more than the destination.

There will be times when you do have to surge or put forth an extraordinary amount of effort to meet a deadline or complete a project; just remember to compensate.

Remember, as with the scale, the bicycle, and the airplane, when a force acts to put you out of balance, an opposite and equal force must be applied to compensate. There will be times when you do have to surge or put forth an extraordinary amount of effort to meet a deadline or complete a project. I get it. But just remember the scale—compensate for the imbalance. If you do this, you will ensure that you can sustain a healthy life and business, come what may.

PRINCIPLE 1

When we focus on nothing else but pursuing the dream, leaving all else aside, we do serious harm to ourselves and those we love and care deeply about. It is critical that you maintain a balance between your personal and business lives.

CHAPTER EIGHT

Don't Buy It Unless You Need It

"It's what goes on between your ears that will determine your decisions and therefore your spending actions."

ONE OF THE GREAT challenges in any business, whether a startup or long-running business, is sufficient resources—or the lack of sufficient[9] resources.[10] In fact, you could argue that's a challenge in most any situation or organization. But it's especially true in the startup phase of a new business or project.

When I say resources, you probably think I'm referring to cash. Of course, you'd be right, but I'm not only referring to cash. I'm also referring to people, equipment, technology, raw materials, infrastructure like offices, warehouses, transportation assets, and so forth—everything you need to deliver your product or service.

---

9 US Chamber of Commerce, February 25, 2019, "We Ask: What's Your Biggest Challenge? Entrepreneurs Say It's Financing," retrieved August 1, 2019 from https://www.uschamber.com/co/run/business-financing/business-financing-challenges

10 Deluxe Enterprise Operations, LLC, "Top 10 Challenges Faced By Entrepreneurs Today: Solved" retrieved August 1, 2019 from https://www.deluxe.com/sbrc/financial/top-10-challenges-faced-entrepreneurs-today-solved

Not having the resources you need, when you need them, will bring your whole business to a screeching halt.

So, is the problem just having enough cash and stuff, or just doing a better job of planning? While the stuff is important, I don't believe it's the biggest problem. If it were, you could probably deal with shortfalls or deficiencies quickly and keep moving. But as with most things in your life, the battlefield isn't usually the cash or stuff you need. The battlefield is usually in the mind, not in the resources. How you think trumps everything. Are you thinking correctly about your resource needs?

"How you think trumps everything."

What do I mean? It's what goes on between your ears that will influence your decisions, your plans, and therefore your spending actions. It is extremely helpful if you've already thought about what your plan for your resources will be before you arrive at the decision or problem. How much can you spend? How much should you spend? A budget would be really useful, of course. But even after you've set a budget, you still have to decide on when and how much to spend as needs arise. It's the execution of the budget I want you to consider. A budget is only a plan and is only as good as the one executing it.

Now, I don't want to make this difficult. I only want to give you some thoughts to consider. Here's some proven advice I've used to aid my decision-making when it comes to executing my budget or getting things I need for my business. I call this the "Entrepreneur's Spending Rules." I know it's not a very creative title, but it's also not confusing.

Entrepreneur's Spending Rules

1. Don't buy it until you need it. Use some real discipline here. Ask yourself, "What impact will it have if I wait to buy this item? Do I absolutely need it now? Will this help me generate more income, or will it just lower my profits?" And the real

question: "Is this a want or a need?" Be brutally honest with yourself. Phone a friend if needed.

2. If you need it, don't hesitate to buy it. Having said all of that, if you do need this item, don't hesitate. If it will help you generate more income, open more opportunity, make you more efficient, save you time so you can focus on more income-generating activity, then *don't hesitate*! Buy it!

3. But make sure you need it. Go back to the first rule above and ask yourself once more, "But do I really need it?" In my experience, most of the time there are ways to get things done without spending money, or as much money, as you think you need.

Years ago, my small business operating model called for the use of a shared office space. It was ideal. All of my employees worked from home. The included shared office services provided a corporate mailing address in a nice part of the city, an answering service with our own phone number, and access to conference rooms as needed. We could also rent office space when needed. The most wonderful thing is that we only paid for what we used. This kept our costs down to hundreds of dollars per month, versus thousands to actually lease and furnish a space. What could be better?

Over the years, business went well for us, and we experienced significant growth. It began to feel like we needed our own office space. We were using the shared space more and more, which was a bit pricey. It was fine when we only used it once a week or so, but the pricing for the service actually wasn't designed for it to be used regularly. So as we used it more and more, the costs began to approach the cost of leasing our own space. That led me to begin looking into an office lease.

We found a very nice office in a beautiful building. It gave a very professional impression. It was in a great location near public transportation, restaurants, hotels, bars, and other services nearby. However, there were two problems: it was pricey and twice as big as we needed. One side of my brain was saying, "You need this office space. It is so prestigious and beautiful. It'll let others know you're successful." And the other side was saying, "Ouch! The cost is really high. You don't need this. You could find another place a mile away to reduce the cost. Yes, it's not as prestigious or near things, but so what? You could also keep things as they are." I went back and forth, and back and forth. If I'm honest, my pride or ego was overly influencing my thinking—a very dangerous mindset to be in. The prideful side of my brain was saying, "Okay, it's pricey, but you can afford it. Your business is only going to grow, so it'll soon be easily affordable." The logical side said, "Yes, but what if things go south and the business shrinks? You'll be locked in a five-year lease and in real trouble."

I'm ashamed to say I let the prideful side of my brain win the argument. Things went well for several years as we did continue to grow. But then the recession hit and we took big losses. The lease began to be a real problem, and we still had eighteen months left on it. Our office was now way too big for our needs and our revenue. I had no choice but to try to negotiate my way out of the lease, costing me lots of money in attorney fees and administrative costs. Again, if I'm honest, we could have either moved to a less expensive location or signed a shorter lease or kept the shared office model and come out much, much better financially. It was an expensive lesson.

Now whenever I'm considering spending or committing to something big or expensive, I use my "Entrepreneur's Spending Rules" and give myself time to step back, seek counsel from a mentor or partner, and try to remove the emotion or pride from the decision—to be as objective and honest with myself as I can. This has worked much, much better and helped me avoid costly mistakes.

• • •

One more thing: avoid debt like the plague. Granted, debt can be a good thing for a business, so I'm not totally against it. In my mind, there is good debt and bad debt. For example, if debt is required to purchase something that will definitely generate more income for you, then that's good debt, and I'm less resistant to it. But if the debt is only for an expense that won't generate income for you, then that's bad debt, and I'm totally against it. I'm a huge believer in bootstrapping—paying for things with available cash. If you take a hard look around you, at your current assets and resources, you might be amazed at what you can do with your own resources and just a little creativity.

I recommend you read *Stretch* by Scott Sonenshein, a brilliant book on achieving more with less. It is an easy read, but it will challenge your thinking in the area of spending.

> ***"... you don't usually make purchasing errors when buying the expensive things (computers, copiers, furnishings); it's the everyday expenses ... that can really add up and chip away at your profits."***

You might say, "Wayland, you're making much too big a deal out of this." What I hope you'll see is that if you get yourself and your employees thinking along these lines of the rules I've given you, you'll be absolutely amazed at what you really need to operate your business successfully. And let me point out that, in my experience, you don't usually make purchasing errors when buying the expensive things (computers, copiers, furnishings); it's the everyday expenses that most folks don't focus on that can really add up and chip away at your profits. So use my rules for ongoing, everyday expenses, too.

Remember, it's not what you make, but what you keep.

PRINCIPLE 2

Don't buy it unless you need it. If you need it, don't hesitate to buy it. But make sure you need it. Be honest with yourself. And avoid debt like the plague. Use your own resources first.

CHAPTER NINE

Uncertainty: How Will You Respond?

"It's not a matter of if *things will go wrong, but* when *things will go wrong."*

ONE OF THE MOST difficult things small business owners and entrepreneurs have to contend with each day is risk or uncertainty. What are the risks to the business? Where are they? How big are they? Assuming one cannot eliminate risk, what is an acceptable level? And maybe the biggest question, how can you mitigate or lessen your risk? The question is not *if* things will go wrong or against you, but *when* things will go wrong or against you.

Who can know the future? We can only make educated guesses about it. We can size up our competition, market conditions, examine our past costs in an attempt to predict future costs, but there is no guaranteed method to predict the future or the risk. We only know what we know. As mentioned earlier, and worth repeating, former Secretary of Defense Donald Rumsfeld is famous for saying, "There are known knowns. These are things we know that we know. There are known unknowns. That is to say, there are things that we know we don't know. But there are also unknown unknowns. There are things we don't know we don't know." It's that last bit—unknown unknowns—that keeps business owners up at night.

Even though it's impossible to be 100 percent accurate, I'm a big believer in going through a planning process to try to understand what the future might hold for your business. What follows is the simple process I use to gain insight into the future of my company. I encourage you to use it as a starting point for creating your own planning process for your company.

1. Write down all the risks to your business you can think of: marketplace competition, a slowing economy, insufficient cashflow, employee challenges such as lack of talent or unexpected departures, and whatever else you can think of for your situation.

2. Next, synthesize all of these risks and try to create several scenarios that would impact your business. For example, a competitor challenges you directly through aggressive pricing and poaching a key employee. Or perhaps a slowing economy causes you to cut costs and delay bonuses, which causes a key employee to leave. Another approach is to ask yourself the question, "What could possibly go wrong?" Don't limit your thinking at this point, even if your scenarios are a bit wild. Get all these scenarios sketched or outlined on paper. Plus, don't forget to think about what you would do if your business suddenly experienced explosive growth! This last scenario also requires a lot of thinking and planning so that you're prepared for success. I'd hate to win a large contract, then sub-optimize the results because I wasn't ready! That would really hurt.

3. Rank all of your scenarios from "most likely" to "not very likely." Then from that list, make an honest assessment of the scenarios that concern you the most, the ones that you think are most likely and impactful if you're unprepared—the ones

that keep you up at night. These we'll call your critical planning scenarios.

4. For each critical planning scenario, you must develop a reasonable response that would address the most critical aspects. Most of the time your responses will include identifying backup sources of cash or other resources to sustain you through troubles—cash being the most likely resource you'll need, but not the only one. You might need a plan to find and hire talent or a plan to acquire needed equipment or temporary third party support until you put a more permanent solution in place. You and your team will need to craft a response to each scenario that is actionable, within your capability and resources, and resolves the problem.

By using a simple planning process like this, you'll gain a much better understanding of your business, your market, your competitors, what your capabilities are, your strengths, and your weaknesses. You'll be much better prepared for the future than before.

"Money costs money, unless it's yours already."

Speaking of cash, the good thing about it is that it has the potential to solve a lot of your troubles—not all, but a great deal. The bad thing about cash is that when you're in a crisis, it is often the most elusive of resources unless you have planned for it. You have to realize that money costs money, unless it's already yours. If you rely upon a credit line for emergencies, that's all well and good, but you'll pay for it. However, if you've put money aside during the good times, it should cost you nothing to obtain and use it because you already have it.

One critical thing to note: if you don't have a credit line already, you won't be able to get one when you are in trouble. You must get a credit line set up when it is *not* needed. I know, I know—but that's how banks work.

Here are four essential tips to consider when planning your cash requirements for "unknown unknowns":

1. Put money aside during the good times. Pay yourself (your firm) first, then everyone else (your suppliers). Whatever is left should be put aside. If you don't have anything left after paying yourself and everyone else, then there's a bigger question you need to ask yourself: "Why not?" You obviously need to make some adjustments, either increase your revenues or reduce your expenses. Breaking even each month is not sustainable. Without that extra margin, you'll never be ready, nor able to even get ready, for a rainy day. It is essential you make a sufficient margin. Do whatever you have to, but get and keep that margin.

2. Set up a credit line when you're in the good times. You will *not* be able to set one up when trouble hits. Don't abuse this credit line, but use it only as an essential tool for cashflow problems—a temporary answer to cashflow problems. Pay the credit line off immediately.

3. Identify alternative sources of cash in your response plans: your own personal resources, family, or friends. You may have to be creative. Don't rely only on credit.

4. Don't bet what you can't afford to lose. If it all goes wrong, you must be able to carry on despite your losses. When you create your response plans for the likely scenarios you may face, be sure you can carry on, regardless. If you cannot, then serious thought has to be given to the risks you are taking. Ask yourself, "What would I have to do to keep operating if it all went wrong?"

Let Me Repeat: Create Margin for Error

My final thought is that as entrepreneurs, we will take chances—hopefully, well-informed chances. It's what we do. We are the innovators and creators who bring the best ideas to the market. But as you do this—and don't stop doing it, by the way—give yourself a chance for success by creating margin in your business. You must allow for "unknown unknowns." If you have no margin for error, you are on a fool's errand. It's only a matter of time before you hit a wall. Make sure you can adapt and survive.

PRINCIPLE 3

It's not a matter of *if* things will go wrong, but *when*. Remove uncertainty and discover more about your business, market, and customer through planning, creating responses to likely scenarios you may face in business. Ensure you include margin for error.

CHAPTER TEN

Should I Consider Debt for My Small Business?

"Yes, debt can be very dangerous used unwisely. But the truth is debt can be a good thing, too."

I DON'T THINK THERE is anything more frightening to the entrepreneur or small business owner than the thought of going into debt. When you put your personal assets up as collateral, as small business owners often have to do, it's hard not to be a little nervous or uncertain. I've laid in bed many nights with scary thoughts dancing through my head of collection agents coming to my home or receiving certified mail notifying me of the lender's intent to take my assets away because I couldn't repay a debt.

Yes, debt can be very dangerous if used unwisely. But the truth is debt can be a good thing, too. I've heard story after story about entrepreneurs who started out with a small loan and ended up with an incredible business. Take Kevin O'Leary, founder of O'Leary Financial Group, for example. His mother loaned him $10,000 to start his business out of his basement. Fast forward many years later, and he sold his business for $4 billion.[11] I am not suggesting that everyone

---

11 O'Leary, K. (2016, April 7). 3 Ways To Grow Your Cashflow With Debt. Retrieved from: www.inc.com.

will see that kind of success, but you get my point. Kevin had to go into debt to have a chance at success.

What Goes on Between Your Ears

So, yes, debt can be a good thing. It can also be the thing that brings your business to a sad end. In my experience, the most significant contributor to the poor use of debt in small businesses, and your personal life, for that matter, is a wrong state of mind regarding debt—what goes on between your ears. We allow our emotions to affect our thinking, which affects our financial decisions—not good.

As Jonah Lehrer puts it in his book *How We Decide*, "While the emotional brain is capable of astonishing wisdom, it is also vulnerable to certain innate flaws. These are the situations that cause the horses in the human mind to run wild so that people gamble on slot machines and pick the wrong stocks and run up excessive credit card bills."[12] If we can remember that we are flawed human beings subject to emotional fits of idiocy, then we have a chance to keep ourselves from disaster, and not just in the area of finances.

The entire previous section of this book is devoted to our thinking because it's so critical. We make so many mistakes because we are thinking about a problem incorrectly. First, we often don't see or know everything, so when making important decisions, we must take the time needed to make sure we have the full picture in front of us. This first step is critical. If you don't have sight of the full situation, everything you do going forward will be handicapped. After you have sight of the full situation, then you must do all you can to make sure you understand what you're looking at.

Many times I've had a good full view of the problem but misunderstood what was actually happening. Talk to associates, partners, or good friends about the problem. Ask those actually in

12 [2] Mourdoukoutas, P. (2012, November 24). Good Debt Bad Debt. Retrieved from www.forbes.com.

touch with the problem, who are closest to it, to tell you what they believe is happening. Finally, after you've made sure you have full view of the problem and understand what you're looking at, give yourself the time needed to let your decision mature—what you're going to do. I've made the mistake of putting unnecessary time pressure on myself to make a decision when there was no need to rush. When you allow time for the decision to "percolate," the best answers usually rise to the top or make themselves obvious. You'll get a sense of what is best. There is a proverb that says, "Let peace act as the umpire in all decisions you make." In other words, you'll know you have your answer when you have that sense of peace. You've done your due diligence; now let the decision mature or ripen until you have peace about the direction you should take. This approach has worked for me, time and time again.

Okay, back to the subject of debt.

Good Debt vs. Bad Debt

Good debt helps you—it creates an asset or generates income. Using a simplistic example to make my point, let's say you won a one-year contract for $30,000 to cut lawns in your large neighborhood. You find an industrial-grade mower that can easily and quickly do the job for $3,000, but you're short on cash. You borrow the $3,000 to buy the mower, and assuming you pay $3,000 to operate and maintain the mower all year, you will make a gross profit of $24,000. To me, this would be a good use of debt because it generates income and creates an asset, the mower.

Bad debt hurts you—it does not create an asset or income, but only creates an expense. Let's say you discover some beautiful office furniture and it's been reduced in price, though it's still pretty expensive. Your current furniture is in great shape, looks professional, is very functional, but is not the latest trend in office design look and feel. You love the look of the new furniture, and you tell yourself this furniture will help improve employee morale, make you more competitive because it looks so cool and customers will love it, and the price has been reduced even though it's still steep. You would have to borrow the money to buy the furniture because the whole office would need to be outfitted since it's so different from your current furnishings.

> ***"Rather go to bed without dinner than to rise in debt."***
>
> **—Benjamin Franklin**

In my opinion, even though the furniture is an asset, this is bad debt because it is not an income-generating asset—nor is it something that could be sold off easily for the amount needed to repay the loan. This loan will not result in any income or increase of your worth.

Did you note the emotions in this scenario and how they were used to rationalize the decision-making process? It's classic emotional thinking, putting us in the wrong state of mind. Now, I'm not against keeping the office environment looking professional and improving employee morale, but it should be done with available cash, not a loan. Save the money, then buy the furniture. Or cool off a bit and let this decision have time to mature. You might discover you don't need this furniture after all. Put the money into employee training or business development to generate more revenue.

With any major purchase, ask yourself the hard question: "Do I really need it? Would this create good debt or bad debt?" And be honest. If you don't trust yourself, then ask someone you know that will be brutally honest.

PRINCIPLE 4

When considering debt, be honest and ask yourself hard questions. Consider whether it's good debt or bad debt—will it increase your income or worth? If not, avoid it like the plague.

CHAPTER ELEVEN

The Most Critical Business Skill You Have

"At the end of the day people won't remember what you said or did, they will remember how you made them feel."

—Maya Angelou

WHEN I FIRST STARTED out in business, my main focus was on the delivery of my services. I thought that if I got that right, then my company was sure to win. After all, why am I being paid if not to deliver what I said I would deliver, on time and budget? You may be thinking similar thoughts, that it's the business of business that's key to the game. Get it right, and all else will fall into place.

I couldn't have been more wrong. At some point, I finally realized that my customer wasn't only buying my services; they were also buying me. Others in my market could do similar services, offer similar deliverables, but no one else offered me. I was the only one that could offer me. My client wanted my services, but they also wanted me, my thinking, my leadership, my influence, my approach to their needs. Their confidence was in me.

This idea can also extend to one or more of your valuable employees. The bottom line is that it's the relationship that's most critical, and your ability to establish, build, and cultivate that relationship is the most critical business skill you have.

You might say, "I don't deliver services. I make widgets, so I am less dependent on my relationship skills." Be honest with yourself. Yes, it might be that you make wonderful widgets, but isn't the relationship you've built with that client what brought the business in the door?

How much of the iPhone market share was about Steve Jobs? Yes, Apple has great products, but you and I both know Steve Jobs added a tremendous value to the product—almost a cult-like following from Apple customers. Would the iPhone be the same without Steve Jobs? Would it have sold the same without him? Do you see my point? You may sell widgets, but you are still critical to the product and its success.

Relationship Skills Are More Critical Than Business Skills

Your business relationships and your relationship skills are *more* critical than your business skills—marketing, finance, etc. Show me a person with average business skills but outstanding relationship skills, and I'll show you a person who *will* succeed. Show me a person with average relationship skills but outstanding business skills, and I'll show you a person who *might* succeed.

> ***"Show me a person with average business skills but outstanding relationship skills, and I'll show you a person who*** will ***succeed. Show me a person with average relationship skills but outstanding business skills, and I'll show you a person who*** might ***succeed."***

Maybe you're thinking, "Okay, I agree with you, but what can I do to improve my relationship skills?" Glad you asked. There are many, many things you can do, and entire books have been written on the subject, but below are just a few quick tips from me to help you get started. As you move forward in developing these skills, write down the things you learn along the way. It will help to confirm and solidify what you've learned and highlight what skills you still need to improve.

1. Decide. First, you must agree that relationship skills are the most critical business skill or asset you have and must continually develop. Some of you are struggling already with this idea. However, before we can go any further, you have to decide that this is critical. Business is all about relationships. You may think it's first about profits, cashflow, sales and marketing, but those are all secondary to relationships. This is foundational—everything else is built upon it.

2. Desire to Improve. Second, you have to want to improve this skill, and yes, it is a skill, and yes, you can improve it. Many of you will see this as a "soft" skill or something that's "nice to have" but is not critical. You're more interested in the technical skills of finance, marketing, process improvement, etc. These are all great skills, but if your relational skills are well developed, all of the technical skills will be exponentially more impactful than without them.

3. Commit to Learn. Learn what you can from noted thought leaders on the subject of relationship skills. To start you out, let me suggest Dale Carnegie's *How to Win Friends and Influence People*. This is a business classic, having sold over thirty million copies. Additionally, search the internet for podcasts or video with content by experts on relationships.

4. Get a Mentor. Find someone who is very good at relationships, who is successful, someone who is easy to talk to, someone who makes you smile and cares about you. Bring this topic to them. Ask them how they feel about relationship skills and what they could do to help you improve. Sit under their tutelage. Learn all you can.

5. Adopt the Golden Rule. Adopt the Golden Rule, or similar behavioral ethic, to "treat others as you would like to be treated." This rule suggests so much about how we're to treat others—not just our business relationships, but our families and friends, and our competitors and those we find difficult, too. Ouch! Got you with that one, didn't I? You see, anyone can treat those we like with kindness, but what about those who are difficult?

   By the way, I struggle in this area. However, if you can learn this skill, it can open new doors. Once, I was able get past my own negative feelings and treat someone I did not like with respect. Unexpected opportunities emerged with this person and went so well that we are now friends doing great business together. If I had not treated them by the "Golden Rule," I would have missed not only a big opportunity for business but also what is now a great friendship. And if I'm honest, I still struggle with this relationship, but my relationship skills keep everything working with this person. It's still hard to do, but I know it's the right thing to do.

   After all, one way to get rid of competitors or difficult people is to make them partners or friends. Don't limit your friends or relationships to just the people you align with ideologically or culturally. Open up to those you wouldn't normally, and see what happens. You never know from where your next blessing or fulfilling friendship will come. I've experienced this many times in my life.

6. Remain Teachable. No matter how old or how experienced you become, keep your mind open, your heart compassionate, and consider for one moment that you might not have all the answers. You need people around you, all kinds of people: clients, customers, partners, peers, mentors, employees, family, friends, suppliers, etc. You can't do life or business alone—you

weren't meant to—so don't try. You can't know everything, either; again, you weren't meant to, so don't try. Experience the joy of a community of friends, partners, associates, and family. Don't limit yourself to just you.

You Are in the People Business

No matter who you are or what your business does, you are in the people business. Therefore, relationship skills are critical. The quote at the beginning of this article by Maya Angelou is so true. It's how you make people feel that is most important, not what you said or did, and not how good your service or product is. Do you make people feel good? Safe? Happy? Content?

Lastly, if you can cultivate your relationship skills, not only will you thrive, but you will be better able to survive when things go wrong. Anyone can do well when things are going great. The real test of your business, your life, and your character is how well you do when things go wrong. I would not have survived my tough years if I had not had those special relationships with family, friends, and those in and around my business—no way. Not only did I survive the tough times, I thrived. You can, too, if you practice cultivating your relationships.

PRINCIPLE 5

Your relationships and relationship skills are *more* critical than your business skills. Cultivate and improve them to ensure sustained success and happiness—in life and business.

CHAPTER TWELVE

Survival: How to Crush It in a Downturn

"Companies that model best practices, that model the most upstanding principles, end up as the most profitable. It's not a trade of profits versus principles."

—Philip Zimbardo

ANYONE CAN LEAD A business or organization when things are going well. However, leading in a downturn when revenues are falling, when demand is low and profits suffer, is an entirely different matter. If you've run your business with sound principles and practices, you are more prepared and likely to survive.

During the last recession, my consulting business experienced tremendous downward pressures from increased competition coupled with fewer opportunities. It was much harder to get work, and the work that I did get had much lower margins due to the aggressive pricing I was forced to use to be competitive. Add to that my existing fixed costs and the financial problems were even worse.

The good news is that I did survive. In fact, I went on to thrive, even in the downturn. Before the downturn, I had made some strategic decisions in my business, not with a recession or downturn in mind but as good principled decisions. I made those choices because I thought it prudent and beneficial. It turns out it was more than that. Those choices positioned me to survive and to go on and thrive. If you truly do what's right for your business every day based on proven practices, you should be ready for most any challenge that comes.

My Business Survival Tips for the Downturn

So, what did I do? Below are the things I chose to do, along with other things I should have done had I been thinking about strategies to protect my business in a downturn. You get the full advantage of my hindsight. These aren't the only things you can do, but this is a great "think piece" for anyone and will apply to most any business.

1. <u>Become the best at one thing</u>. Especially when you are a small business, specializing in one product or service area is the smart play. Be known for it. Having too many offerings raises your overhead, spreads your resources out too thin, and causes a lack of focus on your core strengths. It can even confuse your customer as to what your business is all about. I can understand why you might want to offer a wide variety of things, hoping to capture as much business as possible, or you may think it spreads your risk by making you more diverse. But when the competition gets fierce and the margins thin, a narrow and deep offering beats a wide and thin one every time. Your customer should easily know what you're all about. Decide on that "one thing" you excel in, and then be the very best. In my case, my customers called on me during the recession because when they needed what I offered, I easily came to mind first. This was critical to our survival. Oh, sure, you may still want to have the ability to offer other things, but keep your main thing clearly the main thing.

2. Cultivate close partnerships and alliances. Form and cultivate close partnerships and alliances with companies with whom you fit well. For example, don't cozy up to someone who is a competitor or in your same product space. Find those firms and individuals that complement you and vice versa. This is a long-term process, but so worth it. Just like in tip number one above, not only did my customer think of me first, but my partners also thought of me first when a need arose because we complemented each other, and I was the best at the one thing they needed.

3. Strengthen your cash position and self-finance. When margins get thin, and revenues decline, you need to be able to use your own cash and resources. This keeps your overhead low. I had to decline a major contract once because the margins were thin and I couldn't get affordable financing, even with a signed contract. If I'd had the cash on hand, I would have been able to self-finance, do the work, and make a profit. Build up your cash in the good times so you can self-finance. If you wait until you need the cash, you might not be able to get it.

4. Invest in your most critical people. During the last downturn, being able to retain my best people was critical. I had invested in them over time and enjoyed their total loyalty to me and our business. Identify and cultivate your "franchise players." When things get tough, you need to know your best people are with you, no matter what. And when I say invest in them, I'm not just talking about salaries, benefits, and other incentive programs. Invest yourself in them, too. They need to feel connected to you and your business.

5. Keep your overhead low. This should go without saying, but I've still seen this as a basic problem with small businesses. Buy only what you need. Don't hesitate to get it if you need it. But

make sure you need it. See my other chapter in this book for more tips in the area of spending. Oh, and avoid bad debt like the plague. See my other chapter on this topic, too.

6. Be prepared to make compassionate but tough choices. When you are in a downturn, you will have to make tough choices. It's unavoidable if you're to survive. Renegotiating contracts, leases, and supplier agreements will certainly be necessary. Parts of your business may need to be shut down. But where it gets really tough is when you have to make personnel decisions like laying people off, moving some people from full-time to part-time salary, and skipping bonuses and pay raises. This is where you need your loyal employees to help you keep things from going into a death spiral. By far the biggest mistake owners make in this situation is *not* making a key personnel decision soon enough that will help keep their business afloat. Read Dr. Henry Cloud's book *Necessary Endings*. It was a tremendous help to me when I had to make these kinds of tough choices. It helped me see these kinds of decisions in a healthy, compassionate way. I was able to do what was best for the business and the remaining employees. He changed my thinking completely in this area.

7. Broaden your customer base. I've suggested in tip number one to specialize and be the best at one thing. But don't limit your customers to one. Said another way, diversify your client base, not your services. Cultivate as many customers as you can. Seek out customers in diverse markets and industries. For example, I was mainly in the government contracting space but began offering my services to private firms in many other markets and industries. It resulted in additional work. I love having a broad range of customers in diverse markets. I think it makes your business more stable and survivable, not to mention more valuable.

8. Monitor customer and market trends. Get out there in the market and meet new people, read new books and articles, go to conferences to hear and meet thought leaders, see what everyone is talking about. Even if everything is running great, you're one trend away from being marginalized or obsolete. Stay ahead of your competitors. Your ability to see trends and innovate, or not, will determine your future viability. As my old Navy captain once told me, "Keep your head on a swivel, Wayland. You never know where the next challenge or opportunity is coming from."

9. Stay teachable and keep learning. Related to tip number eight above is to stay teachable. Consider that you don't know everything, no matter how experienced you are, no matter how many college degrees you have, no matter how many books you've written. When my son came to work for me, he taught me so much about managing millennials. I didn't want to accept it at first. After all, I had been in business many years and knew how to manage people, right? But after stumbling and embarrassing myself a few times, I had to admit that he knew things I didn't. My mistake was to think that I had arrived and needed no further help in people management and leadership, especially from my son. I was wrong. Don't stop learning. Try to consider that you may not have all the answers and need help.

10. Keep your life in balance. During the recession, if I had not maintained a balance between life and the business with the support of my spouse, family, and close friends, I would not have survived. You must keep a balance between your business and your life. One affects the other. They are not independent, but interdependent. They must be managed together. To constantly focus only on your business is like starving your body of a balanced diet. You will get sick. You will not be healthy. You will not be able to fight off disease well.

PRINCIPLE 6

Learn and practice good business practices and life principles. If you truly do what's right for your business and life every day, based on proven practices and principles, you will be ready for most any challenge that comes.

CHAPTER THIRTEEN

Employees: My Top Management Insights for Owners

My experience has shown that employee skills and expertise can be developed, but character cannot.

FOR MOST BUSINESSES, THERE is no greater asset than your employees. Of course, there can be no greater liability, too. If you've got people of great character and talent, they are likely worth every penny and more. They are the secret sauce to a successful business and a rewarding experience as a small business owner. If you've got the wrong people, however, of no character or talent, with caustic attitudes bringing harmful chemistry in the workplace, it can seem like your worst nightmare for both yourself, your other employees, and your clients or customers.

Getting the composition of your team right is essential. It is likely something that could make or break your business. Many books have been written on this subject. Many firms consult on this issue. A considerable portion of your overhead is probably allocated to your employees. Whatever amount of time or resources you spend to get the employee question right is perhaps one of the best uses of your resources, no question.

I will not pretend to be complete or comprehensive in this short chapter. However, I do offer my insights for your consideration, which have come from my years as a small business employer. Use what makes sense to you.

My Top Insights on Employee Management

1. Hire on character. My experience has shown that employee skills and expertise can be developed, but character cannot. When I say character, I mean personality, disposition, temperament, ethics, chemistry, and their general nature. It is possible to influence one's character, but it pretty much stays however you first found it. I've hired people with impressive skill sets only to be disappointed later due to workplace problems related to their character. This usually ends with me letting them go. Conversely, I've hired people with minimal skills but strong character and was almost never disappointed. How do I determine a candidate's character? After confirming the minimum qualifications and references of the candidate, we spend time with them socially as part of our interview process. In this way, we try to get to know who they are. We sometimes still make hires we regret, but more often than not, we get it right. The team I currently have is the most fantastic set of professionals I've ever had.

2. Watch those salaries. Carefully set your wages based on your revenue and profit targets. Don't let them get too high, especially when the employee is first hired. When you make an offer to a potential employee, make sure you can live with it. If it is rejected, move on and don't look back. Do your best research on what the position is worth. Many websites have

detailed salary information for your location. Sometimes your business partners will share salary info with you, too. Use all available information to guide you, but you need to set your salaries based on your situation. Make sure your salary levels leave room for pay raises and bonuses. And remember there are other ways to compensate your employees besides financially: individual recognition awards given out in public, gifts, training and conferences, off-site social time together, time off, and so on. Like you, I want to compensate my people fairly. I want them to feel properly treated. But you can't please everyone, so don't try. Do your best. No one can ask for more.

3. Keep a healthy culture. I like to compare a healthy workplace culture to a healthy garden. To keep a healthy garden, you must continuously work the soil, keeping it tilled, free of weeds, properly fertilized, and watered. If you do this, you will enjoy the benefits of beauty and nourishment. Similarly, a healthy workplace culture requires proper attention and cultivation. You want to create the conditions for healthy relationships, good communication between workers and management, a sense of fairness to all, and a work ethic that balances the needs of the company and the individual. When an employee is "planted" in your workplace garden, you want to know you have created the conditions for them to have everything they need to succeed, personally and professionally. If you do this well, like with the garden, you will reap the benefits of both beauty and nourishment. It starts with the leader, or to continue the analogy further, the gardener. So how does your garden grow?

4. Don't delay tough choices. One mistake I've made is to take too long in dismissing an employee or delivering other forms of bad news, such as a failure to promote or a poor performance review. It is a difficult thing to do. It should be

difficult. If it weren't difficult, I'd worry about your lack of human compassion. I've learned over the years, however, that by delaying the tough choices, I am probably causing more problems. For example, when ending someone's employment, you may be doing them a favor by allowing them to pursue other, more lucrative opportunities. It happened to me, so I know this to be true. Moreover, by delaying a poor performance review, you perpetuate the problem rather than giving the employee the gift of an opportunity to improve. Delaying bad news isn't like fine wine; it does not get better with age. Be strong, take courage, and do what you know is right. It's better for everyone.

5. Enjoy your team. Ask any professional athlete who has been part of a winning team if they enjoyed their experience. They always say yes. When you carefully assemble and maintain your team, cultivate a healthy culture, and work together toward shared goals, you always enjoy yourself. Treat your team like you'd want to be treated; show empathy for others, clearly communicate your vision, cultivate an atmosphere of openness and fairness, encourage an ethos of constant learning and improvement, and I believe you'll see everyone enjoying his or her time at work. Who wouldn't want to work in an environment like that? So, enjoy your team, and they will enjoy working for you.

PRINCIPLE 7

Employee skills can be developed. Character cannot. Make every effort to hire well. Take the time it deserves because it's essential to get it right.

CHAPTER FOURTEEN

Making Better Decisions for Your Business

"Let peace be the umpire for all your final decisions."

—Proverb

MANY TIMES I'VE HAD difficult business and personal decisions to make, some of them quite important. Most of the time those decisions were not split-second, life-or-death decisions requiring immediate action, unlike a paramedic at the scene of an accident or a soldier in combat. I usually had plenty of time to consider what I was going to do. However, I often did not feel that way. I somehow put myself on some kind of fast-ticking clock, thinking I had to make a choice quickly. This frequently led to regretful outcomes that could have been avoided had I waited a bit longer for additional information and insight.

In 2010, the island of Haiti experienced a magnitude 7.0 earthquake.[13] Thousands of Haitians died and thousands were displaced. How many died has been the subject of some disagreement, but safe to say this was one of thc most devastating events in Haiti's history. The country's

13 Pallardy, Richard (Jan 15, 2010), 2010 Haiti Earthquake, Retrieved from URL: https://www.britannica.com/event/2010-Haiti-earthquake

infrastructure was demolished: public buildings, their airport and seaport facilities, electrical power knocked out, and so on. Even to this day, many years later, the country has not fully recovered.

Haitian ambassador Raymond Joseph was tasked with trying to assist with the emergency response from the United States. This was a daunting task. The first problem was trying to get an accurate assessment of the damage so that a meaningful response could be developed. Communications were almost nonexistent in the beginning. Conflicting reports were constantly coming out of Haiti. There were many people and organizations with great intentions, but there was no single source of knowledge or awareness of conditions in Haiti. Just exactly who was there, what they had brought, what kind of help was underway—it was all chaotic. Planes carrying supplies would land without warning, and often those supplies would sit on the tarmac for days because no one knew the help was there. The left hand didn't know what the right hand was doing.

After some weeks, a picture slowly began to develop of the entire situation. It wasn't a completely accurate picture, but it was reasonable enough to use for planning purposes. It became obvious that one badly needed item was a logistics support plan. This plan would address how people and resources would flow into the country, what resources were needed most, who on the ground there would distribute the resources and to where, and which areas would get help first. Access to and from the air and seaports needed to be coordinated so the traffic flow into and out of Haiti could be managed properly. Where would resources be staged? A security plan for the material was needed to keep it from being pilfered so that it could be made available to the most critical areas first.

The components of a comprehensive logistics support plan are many, and it takes qualified people to create one. But it can be a real difference-maker in a disaster-response operation such as this, bringing efficiency and effectiveness to chaos and inability.

Well, guess what? Logistics support plans are one of the main things my company does. A very good friend of mine was close to the

Haitian ambassador. He was also aware of my company's capabilities and experience planning large operations. He set up a meeting between myself and the ambassador in Washington, DC. The poor man was incredibly busy under tremendous pressure but saw this as a critical item for the relief effort. As I discussed what my company could do for Haiti by creating this plan, he showed great interest, and our conversation lasted over an hour. He asked me to put together a proposal that he could submit to USAID (United States Agency for International Development), who was making funds available for the disaster response in Haiti.

I wrote the proposal and sent it to the ambassador. My cost estimate was as low as I could make it considering the risk involved. I did not want to make a profit but did allow some margin for unforeseen circumstances. I wanted to do this project mostly out of concern for the suffering people of Haiti. I would have been happy to have delivered a quality plan at my cost. My team and I really wanted to help.

After some days, he sent me a message to say he would very much like us to get started on the plan while the proposal made its way through the bureaucracy, asking if I'd be willing to do that. My first thought was, "Absolutely!" I wanted very much to do what I could to help. But I told the ambassador I would need a couple days to consider his request. My proposed cost estimate was well into six figures. I would need startup cash since I had no real idea how long it would take USAID to fund our project. I went to my banker and explained the situation. I even had the ambassador get on the phone when I met with the bank to confirm his support. My banker was very impressed and wanted very much to help. He said they would make the money available so I could start work whenever I wanted. We both assumed the USAID funding would happen. After all, the ambassador himself was pushing the deal. So my banker was all in and also liked the idea of helping Haiti.

As it happens, the next day I had a meeting with my peers at our regularly scheduled monthly meeting where we discussed ideas, shared problems, shared wins, bounced ideas around, and cultivated our friendship. It was a great group of business owners, and we fed off each other. I brought up my Haiti project for discussion. Most everyone was very excited about it and encouraged me to jump in. One person did not. He pulled me aside and began to tell me about his experience working in the Caribbean Islands on many different kinds of projects, some funded by USAID, some privately funded projects. He explained the risks, mostly around agreements and funding, that went with the business culture in that geographical area.

His advice to me was to wait for the USAID funding approval and get 90 percent of it paid up front or don't do the work! He gave me story after story of how things went bad for him until he learned how to protect himself from wavering support, lack of funds, slow payment of invoices, corruption, local politics, and many other challenges working in this part of the world. He had a very successful business, growing almost every year I'd know him. He was a good friend, and I was convinced his only motivation was my welfare. He wanted me to do the work, since he felt we could help those suffering there, but do it wisely. After discussing it with my wife, Karen, I took some quiet time at home to think it all over.

The next day I told my bank I wouldn't need the money. They asked why, and I told them what I'd learned. I told the ambassador I would do the work only when the funds are made available and only if I got 90 percent of the funds up front. He said he understood my request, that it was not unusual (which surprised me and confirmed my friend's advice), and he would work on it.

Some weeks later, I learned the funding plans were all changed by USAID, and the funds the ambassador was seeking disappeared. All funds were channeled to other support groups and efforts after senior USAID decision-makers got involved. I would have been left holding the bag had I started when the ambassador asked. The project would have been unfinished, and I would have increased my debt with nothing to show for it. I did try to get engaged with others working on the relief efforts but learned there was an "inner circle" of those involved with the business of disaster relief, and I wasn't a member. Needless to say, I was very happy I had not started the work.

• • •

Rushing to a decision is one way we can put ourselves in a bad position, leading to bad decisions. There are other ways we can get into trouble when it comes to decision-making:

1. We don't properly understand the issue or problem, leading us to focus on, and try to solve, the wrong thing.
2. We act without seeking advice or counsel.
3. We act upon poor advice.
4. We let the immediate take precedence over the important.
5. We are overly eager to solve the problem and in our haste make errors.
6. We let our emotions cloud our thinking.

Unfortunately, the above list is from my own mistakes. Over the years, I've allowed all those things to affect me and hinder my decision-making. But let me now offer the following tips—also learned over the years—to help you next time you need to make an important decision:

1. Give the decision time to mature. Do your due diligence, then quiet your mind. You will likely find that the answer presents itself when you least expect it. If there's no legitimate reason to rush, take your time.

2. Keep the main thing the main thing. Let your established purpose, mission, goals, and objectives inform your thinking. If you find you're considering a decision that would not align with your current goals or objectives, question it. Either your

goals are outdated and need adjustment, or your decisions should be brought into alignment with them. Don't ignore any misalignment.

3. Seek advice from proper experts. This is so obvious, right? I put it here for a reason. Additionally, don't let friends speak into a decision they have no expertise in. Well-meaning friends can unknowingly contribute to a poor decision. We have blind spots when it comes to our friends. Talk to the experts. If that expert is a close friend, you might consider finding another one.

4. Ask someone who's previously faced your issue. Someone out there has already experienced what you are now going through. Find them. Talk to them. You'll be amazed how this will open your mind to other alternatives to consider.

5. Do your own research. Don't get lazy and rely on everyone else to do your homework. Nothing will ever replace the insights you get when you do your own work.

6. Do your best to quiet your emotions. This can be difficult, but you must try. You may have to remove yourself from your place of work, change the scenery, the environment, the external influences on your mind and emotions. Do something you enjoy. Spend time with your soul mate. The ability to step away from the emotional forces, to objectively consider your alternatives, is vital.

7. Journal about this decision. When you write about your decision in your journal, you will disentangle your thoughts. This will bring clarity, essential to your decision-making. I do this all the time. I cannot imagine making a big decision without it.

8. Confide in your close, personal soul mate. We all need someone in our lives who cares about us with no hidden agendas other than our welfare. Someone who is honest with us. Discuss your decision with them, even if they know nothing about the issue. Just opening up and "rehearsing" the problem with them will often bring further clarity, confirming your next steps. You may be surprised at the questions they ask—ones you never imagined—opening your mind to possibilities you never considered.

Let Peace Be Your Umpire

By far the most crucial tip above is to give the decision time to mature. The next time you have an important decision to make, slow down. Be patient. The answer will present itself when you quiet your mind. I've already mentioned the proverb that says, "Let peace be the umpire for all your final decisions." That's excellent advice. Do your due diligence, for sure, but once that is done, quiet yourself. The answer will come. You'll know it by the peace you have about it.

PRINCIPLE 8

Give your important decisions time to mature. Quiet yourself and listen. Let peace be your umpire.

CHAPTER FIFTEEN

Stay Teachable Because You Know Nothing

"Leaders who don't listen to others will eventually be surrounded by people who have nothing to say."

—Andy Stanley

SOMETHING PROFOUND HAPPENED TO me about the time I reached forty years of age. I had spent my life working, getting smarter and more experienced. I was successful. I felt like I pretty much had things figured out and was becoming the proverbial "fount of knowledge" for all things in my field. What happened about the time I reached forty, however, was that I realized I knew *nothing*. You see, I had gained enough knowledge and experience to now realize that I knew very little. After I mentioned this to a mentor of mine, they said, "Ah! The beginning of wisdom is when you know enough to realize that you actually know *nothing*."

"The beginning of wisdom is when you know enough to realize that you actually know* nothing.*"

Wait. What? You see, in today's fast-changing, fast-paced world, it's impossible to know everything. The sooner you realize this, the sooner you'll get this wisdom and understand that you need others to succeed. No one person possesses all requisite knowledge in their field. Wisdom would then suggest that you collaborate with others in your field to ensure you know as much as you can to accomplish your work as best you can.

The kind of thing that scares me now is when I meet that person who believes they have most all knowable knowledge in their field and are certain of things. Their certainty scares me. They are an accident or failure waiting to happen. Why do you think surgeons consult with each other, or academics share and listen to other ideas, or musicians listen to other musicians, or artists study other artists? I'd rather work with someone who is less certain and seeks to confirm their ideas before putting them into action than someone who thinks they have it all figured out.

This is more about attitude than anything else. It's easy to reach a point in your life where you think you mostly know it all. If a young employee or new hire came to you one day with a suggestion or idea, you might be tempted to marginalize their input because, after all, what could they possibly say that you haven't thought of already, right? Like Andy Stanley said in the quote at the beginning of this chapter, "Leaders who don't listen to others will eventually be surrounded by people who have nothing to say." If your attitude prevents those around you from saying what they think, offering new ideas, pointing out vulnerabilities, criticizing policy, they will keep their mouths shut. This is the tragedy. Potential losses or calamity that could be avoided will not be avoided. Potentially good ideas to grow and improve your business will be missed. You get my point. It's critical, critical, critical that you keep an open mind, no matter how much you think you know or how much experience you think you have.

So, what can be done to make sure you keep an open mind? Below are some tips I've used to stay teachable:

1. Challenge yourself frequently. Even if just for a moment, consider that you might be wrong or unaware of something. My oldest son, Chris, taught me several times that I did not have the full picture of a problem, or I was missing the point, or I was not aware of a new trend, or I did not understand his generation as well as I'd like to think I did. We butted heads several times when he first started working for me. I was upset that he was so "nonconforming" to our company culture, that he challenged almost everything we did.

   To his credit, he never openly challenged me in public. It was only after he barged into my office and closed the door that he would say, "Dad, I can't stand it. You're clueless about this. Please listen to me." It did not go well between us in the beginning. I was too proud. But, to my credit, after I had some time to quiet myself and think about what he was saying, if I was honest with myself, I realized much of what he was advocating for was indeed right. He and I eventually put our feelings aside and kept the business and its employees as the priority, and we made great things happen. He worked for me seven years, and they were the best professional years of my life. We were a better firm because of his willingness to speak up and my willingness to listen and consider his ideas. He is now working for a global consulting firm, doing very, very well. I'm so proud of him.

2. Make it a point to listen to others you usually *do not* agree with. This is a tough one but for me has opened my mind to many ideas and my business to many opportunities. I have a friend who I respected for their achievements. They were very successful. However, I found myself on the complete opposite side, philosophically, of most anything we discussed. It didn't matter what it was. The only place we found agreement was in our faith, so I tried to keep our conversation on that area to avoid tension.

I found myself in need of advice in the very area in which this person was an expert. I avoided seeking their help for some time but eventually put my feelings aside and sought their help. To make a long story short, they were extremely valuable and helped me accomplish my project well. Our friendship also improved to the point where we are comfortable with each other and now interact frequently. I still have issues with our philosophical differences, but we treat each other respectfully and maintain a good relationship. Beyond the solid friendship, the advice and support I received from them completely opened my mind to other new ideas, making the project I was pursuing much, much better than had I not had the advice. Had I only sought advice from someone I could agree with, my project would have suffered, I would not be a better person, nor would I now enjoy a good friendship. Don't write off those you disagree with. There may be something wonderful waiting for you if you're able to rise above the noise of personal disagreement.

3. Read. Don't ever stop reading or learning. One of the most talented authors alive today is Stephen King. Most people think of Stephen as a horror novelist, and he is that, of course—an amazing horror novelist. But he's also written other very wonderful novels, such as *The Green Mile* and *Firestarter*. He also wrote a book about writing called *On Writing*. It's one of the best ever written on the subject. In the book, Stephen gets very practical, very personal, very down-to-earth. But one thing he said has always stuck with me: "Read as much as you write." He says he writes about three to four hours a day, every morning. He also reads novels almost every afternoon, about fifty novels a year. That means he writes two to three novels a year, plus reads fifty novels a year! He said that he has to read to keep his mind fresh and inspired. It's like a fuel tank.

If you only take fuel out but never refuel, eventually you will run out of fuel. That's how he describes his need to read, that it fuels his work. I think it's the same for you and I, in our lives and work. We all need to read, to refresh our minds, and to refill our tanks. It doesn't matter what you read, as long as it's something of interest to you. While Stephen mostly reads novels, he also reads magazines, blogs, and other material. Last year I was able to read forty-six books. I didn't start out with that goal, but that's where I ended up. I read two-thirds nonfiction and one-third fiction. It wasn't difficult, really. I know it sounds like a lot. But I challenge you to turn off the TV, or social media, and pick up a book. You will not regret it. Make it part of your daily routine.

4. Close your mouth and open your ears. When you're having a conversation, about anything, make a point to talk less and listen more. This is a valuable exercise. Even if it's just a conversation with a friend about gardening, cooking, or anything unrelated to your work or business. And when you listen, try to listen to understand. My problem is that when someone is talking to me, I often will form my response as they are talking. Have you ever done that? That's not real listening. Stop working on your response and just listen.

   One way to ensure you're listening to understand is after the other person has finished talking, say to them, "Let me check my understanding. What I think I heard you say was . . ." Then repeat back to them what they said, as they would say it, not as you would say it. This will have a wonderful impact on them because they will see you're really trying to listen to them, which is always gratifying and good for relationships. After you've received confirmation from them that you have understood their point, then you can respond with your perspective. By the way, you will learn much more using this approach.

My most critical insights have often come from listening to those around me, no matter their age, status, or station. Some of the things said to me were not what I decided to do, but by listening, it sparked other thoughts within my mind, which led to other alternatives that I did use. Had I not listened, I would not have had those new and better ideas.

PRINCIPLE 9

No one person can know it all. Stay teachable. Practice a healthy humility. Listen to understand, not to respond.

CHAPTER SIXTEEN

Know Your Exit Before You Enter

"An ounce of prevention is worth a pound of cure."

—Benjamin Franklin

SOME YEARS AGO, DURING the recession, when one part of my small business began to suffer from significant losses in revenues, I found myself in real trouble: too many fixed costs, few options to address them, and no backup plan. For example, I was stuck in the third year of a five-year office lease—a significant expense in my budget. The lease seemed like a good idea at the time. We were growing and times were good. What I failed to consider sincerely was the "what-ifs" of a lease, such as what if business took a downturn and left me with no way to pay my rent? How would I resolve the situation?

It turns out I was able to resolve this problem by negotiating with my landlord. He proved to be kind and understanding. However, that was by no means a given. It could have gone very differently if he had been difficult and unwilling to help. I had no leverage—he had it all. To this day, I count myself blessed that it resolved amicably.

"I did not consider my exit options before I entered the lease."

Looking back, if I had been objective about it all and considered various business scenarios, I think I would have been a little more hesitant to enter into a five-year deal. I could have negotiated a shorter lease—say two or three years—something more aligned to the length of the contracts I currently held, thereby limiting my exposure. Yes, my rent would probably have been slightly higher, but affordable. Alternatively, I could have chosen a shared office space arrangement with month-to-month leasing. I could also have stayed put in my previous small but very functional and affordable space. The point is this: I did not consider my exit options before I entered the lease, and I put my entire business at serious risk.

Another time, I was considering partnering with a firm to bid on a government contract with the US Army. Actually, there were several other firms wanting us to bid with them, but one in particular looked like it might be better positioned to win than the others. I started a dialogue with this firm. In the beginning, everything felt wonderful. I liked the leadership of this firm. They made a good first impression on me and my team leaders. They were certainly saying all the right things. They wanted to quickly move to signing a teaming agreement. I felt a little rushed. There were many months to go before the bidding process would even start, and I wanted to talk to one or two other firms as part of my due diligence. However, they continued to push to sign an agreement.

With my "know your exit" strategy in mind, I said I would agree to sign if there were "off-ramps" for us should I change my mind. Otherwise, I said I'd rather wait until we knew more about the contract bid, had time to size up the opportunity and competition, and had an agreed work-share arrangement. To my surprise, they agreed to a very low-risk, minimal commitment agreement that gave me complete freedom to walk away. As time passed, it became obvious to me that this firm wasn't what they purported to be. They only wanted our firm for the goodwill we had with the customer, thereby increasing their chances of winning the bid. If we were fortunate enough to win, I had obtained compelling evidence that they intended to cut my work-share sharply once we got started, which I consider a serious integrity breach.

When I confronted the founder of the firm with this knowledge, he denied it at first, but then admitted that was his plan. He said we should feel honored to be on their team and should just accept the situation and move forward. When I said I was pulling out, he threatened legal action. He wasn't fully aware of the terms of the agreement I had negotiated and signed. When he learned that I was free to leave the agreement, he was quite angry with me and his staff. But he could not stop me.

They went on to win the contract without us. So that confirmed my judgment of their position with this client; they were indeed well positioned. But after about a year into the five-year contract, the Army cancelled it for nonperformance. I don't have the details, but the things that got them in trouble had to do with integrity and with nonperformance in the types of things that my firm would have done. For me, the issue of integrity was what caused me to end my relationship with them, and I was glad to have been far away from the damage they had done on the contract. But if I had not had "exit ramps" in my agreement, I may have been legally compelled to continue with the contract, and based on how things went, I believe that our reputation would have suffered as a result.

To be clear, this chapter is not about office leases or contracts. It's about knowing your exit before you enter into anything, whether it's a lease or any other type of contract or business relationship or deal. The best time to find a way to exit a situation that has gone wrong is *not* when you are in the middle of it. By then it is often too late, and you are faced with extreme, and sometimes costly, measures to get yourself out. The best time is at the beginning.

How Do We Get Ourselves Into So Much Trouble?

How do we get ourselves into these situations? Here's what I think:

1. It's easy. It's much easier to get into something than to get out of it. I think it's a law of nature or physics or science or something—in my opinion. We are much better at entering a situation than leaving it. We often let the excitement of the "new thing" blind us to the risks.

2. Hindsight is 20/20. We have perfect hindsight, only seeing the problem after it has occurred. Hindsight can be helpful, yes, but it doesn't get us out of many situations we are already stuck in. It only helps us look back and learn lessons, shutting the barn doors after the cows have already left.

3. Lack of foresight. More helpful than hindsight is foresight: being able to imagine the future—what could go wrong with this decision you are considering. Getting into the habit of using your foresight is the challenge, especially when your emotions are telling you, "Do it. Do it. Do it." But unless you make this part of your thinking or planning process, it usually won't happen because you're so eager to do the "new thing."

How Can We Avoid Trouble in the Future?

Here are the things I do to try to consider the exit before I enter into anything. I still get it wrong sometimes, but when I do, I've been able to significantly reduce my risk and make things manageable when they go against me. Oh, and things will go against you—it's not a question of if, but when.

1. Use scenarios. Try to outline the possible outcomes of a decision you are about to make. What are the different potential

scenarios? Consider all the players, your market, the general economy, new competitors entering your market, available talent, other external forces, and so on. Talk this through with others you trust who are experienced in this sort of thing.

2. Identify exit ramps. Identify the potential "exit ramps" in the scenarios above. How would you get out of the situation you are considering if things went against you? One thing I've learned is that by going through this exercise, I can often create one or more "exit ramps" during this planning stage—but only because I'm doing this now, beforehand. Things can be more easily negotiated or adjusted *before* a deal is reached. It is much harder *after* the deal has been agreed and you are underway.

3. Acceptable risk? Finally, consider your situation if you cannot exit and are stuck with whatever you've agreed. Can you afford to live with it? Can you survive if you lose all of your investment? There may be times when the risk of not doing something is higher than the risk of doing it, and there may be no exit ramp. It's happened to me. I decided I could live with the failure, afford the consequences, and still survive. If you cannot live with the negative consequences, then perhaps this is a risk you should avoid.

Try, Try, and Try Again to Mitigate Risk

I realize there is no way to mitigate away all risk in your business. But that doesn't mean you shouldn't try, try, and try again and only accept the very few and undeniable risks that an entrepreneur must sometimes take if they are to grow, innovate, and succeed. By doing what Benjamin Franklin advised when he was asked about fire safety concerns, you'll understand that "an ounce of prevention is worth a pound of cure."

PRINCIPLE 10

Identify your possible exit points *before* entering into any significant contract or business relationship. The best time to find a way out of a bad situation is *not* when you are already in it.

Part Two Recap: The Top Things I Wish I'd Known Before Starting My Business

PRINCIPLE 1

When we focus on nothing else but pursuing the dream, leaving all else aside, we do serious harm to ourselves and those we love and care deeply about. It is critical that you maintain a balance between your personal and business lives.

PRINCIPLE 2

Don't buy it unless you need it. If you need it, don't hesitate to buy it. But make sure you need it. Be honest with yourself. And avoid debt like the plague. Use your own resources first.

PRINCIPLE 3

It's not a matter of *if* things will go wrong, but *when*. Remove uncertainty and discover more about your business, market, and customer through planning, creating responses to likely scenarios you may face in business. Ensure you include margin for error.

PRINCIPLE 4

When considering debt, be honest and ask yourself hard questions. Consider whether it's good debt or bad debt—will it increase your income or worth? If not, avoid it like the plague.

PRINCIPLE 5

Your relationships and relationship skills are *more* critical than your business skills. Cultivate and improve them to ensure sustained success and happiness—in life and business.

PRINCIPLE 6

Learn and practice good business practices and life principles. If you truly do what's right for your business and life every day, based on proven practices and principles, you will be ready for most any challenge that comes.

PRINCIPLE 7

Employee skills can be developed. Character cannot. Make every effort to hire well. Take the time it deserves because it's essential to get it right.

PRINCIPLE 8

Give your important decisions time to mature. Quiet yourself and listen. Let peace be your umpire.

PRINCIPLE 9

No one person can know it all. Stay teachable. Practice a healthy humility. Listen to understand, not to respond.

PRINCIPLE 10

Identify your possible exit points *before* entering into any significant contract or business relationship. The best time to find a way out of a bad situation is *not* when you are already in it.

PART THREE:

HARD-WON BUSINESS LESSONS THAT WORK

CHAPTER SEVENTEEN

Choosing and Keeping a Partner

"A business partnership can be just like a marriage, either the best or worst thing ever invented in life. Take care who you choose."

"WHY DON'T YOU WANT to work with me?" he asked over my speakerphone. The entire office was listening to this conversation, I was sure. My door was open. Folks had sort of stopped working. They weren't looking my way, but you could tell they were listening. "Because I don't like you!" I said. I shocked myself when I heard those words come out of my mouth, but then I heard chuckles, snickers, and one "yes!" from the others listening in.

That conversation was the end of a courtship where I was trying to decide whether or not to partner with another small business owner I had recently met. At first glance, it looked like a good match. Our two companies weren't redundant. We were each successful. We each offered something unique yet complementary. I felt that we could be stronger together than separate and could put in a very competitive contract proposal to the client. But when we met face-to-face to go over how we would work together, warning signals began to loudly sound.

As the other owner began to talk, the dialogue was all about him, how I should be happy that he "chose" us to partner with him. He said our reputation would only improve working with him and that he was going to obviously win the contract (implying he had an inside track with someone on the client's staff), so we would be wise to agree to his terms and join his team. What I really felt like I was hearing—the unsaid or implied message—was that we had been favored by the king, we should feel grateful to be asked to join his team, and we should willingly accept whatever work-share he deemed fair—and it would probably be appropriate if I felt the desire to kneel and kiss his ring!

My team heard all of this, and I could tell were immediately offended. So was I. But I wanted to *win*! Surely I could put my own ego aside and join forces with this unsavory bum for the sake of a win, right? As a former naval officer, I was taught it's all about the ship, the crew—not your own personal desires. Couldn't I just hold my nose and make the deal and move forward? Isn't revenue growth the main thing?

No, it's not. As you already have seen from the my first sentence above, I chose not partner with him. Why?

Principles trump preferences, every time.

Principles trump preferences, every time. You can negotiate someone's preferences—business rules, work-share, tactics—but you cannot negotiate away someone's principles. This guy was stomping all over my principles of fairness, teamwork, and the golden rule. I knew we would hit an impasse in our relationship—probably sooner than later. Any revenue dreams I might have had would evaporate at that point.

Most mergers fail due to chemistry, according to every expert I know on the subject. It's not the legal or financial aspects of a merger that kill it. The lawyers will have done their jobs, the accountants will have done their jobs. It's the chemistry or culture clashes that kill a merger. I could see our chemistry was not compatible.

So what happened? Well, as you saw, we went our separate ways. This guy did win that contract. And now you're thinking, "Wayland, you made a mistake!" No, I don't think I did. You see, his company was the one I mentioned earlier that got that US Army contract, and his contract was ended early for nonperformance. It appears some of his key employees left his company in the middle of the contract because of toxic working conditions. As a result, his contract performance suffered. His reputation took a big hit. We would have been guilty by association. It's hard not to get mud on you when you're standing next to a child who's stomping in the mud. Choose your partners carefully.

Tips on Choosing a Partner

Choosing a partner in business can be one of the most daunting yet critical things you do as a small business owner or entrepreneur. Whether you are choosing a partner for teaming on a contract proposal effort or choosing a partner for a completely new business offering, or even choosing a partner who will share in the risk and reward of your company, you must approach this decision with clear purpose in a patient, deliberative manner.

In my experience, good partners can be the "secret sauce" to any successful business effort. Partners can also be the death knell to your business. A good partner can make you more competitive, more capable, and more attractive to clients and allies. A bad partnership—well, let's just say it can get pretty ugly. It can be like having a poisonous snake in the garden.

While I don't believe there's any way to completely remove the risk of getting a bad partner, I do believe you can *greatly* reduce the risk. Below are some of my best tips on this subject.

1. <u>Do you need a partner</u>? First, I would start by asking yourself the obvious question: do you really need a partner? Don't just

jump into a partnership because "everyone is doing it." Have clear and compelling business reasons for partnering. You must see that you are better with a partner, or more competitive, or better priced. If you cannot *easily* answer, "Yes" to this question, then stop reading this chapter, pick up the phone, and stop whatever partnership efforts you have underway. Yes, there are risks in going it alone, but they pale in comparison to the pain of a bad partnership.

2. Is there a culture match? Most partnerships, mergers, and acquisitions that go bad do so because of a misaligned culture between the two companies. Ask yourself: Is there a good chemistry between you? Can you get along? Are your cultures similar? For example, if your culture is more aligned with telecommuting and less structured working hours and the partner firm does not believe in telecommuting and enforces a strict work week, you may want to discuss that issue before you agree to a partnership. This is just a simple example and probably shouldn't be the main reason to kill a partnership, but it makes my point about culture. What are your corporate values? Do they match the partner firm's values? For example, if your firm strongly holds a high benchmark on honesty and integrity, it needs to align with another firm with similar values or there will be trouble!

3. Are you redundant? Do your firms mostly offer the same thing to the market? If so, you are redundant. The best situation is where you both offer completely separate services and products. Too much redundancy can bring problems with work-share, market differentiation, pricing, and project management. To the client, a less redundant partnership makes more sense and offers them greater capability. The more redundant partnership will challenge the client to see any benefits from it at all and quite often will confuse the picture.

4. <u>Is there a clear work-share model</u>? After you win the projects or business you're partnering for, will it be clear how the work will be split? If you are not redundant, this will usually be straightforward. If you are redundant, this can get very difficult. In addition, if the partner tends to be agreeable, you can usually work out any work-share differences of opinion. If they tend to be difficult, work-share will bring out the worst in them. Pay attention to personality types in the partner firm. This isn't usually a deal-breaker, but you need to be aware.

5. <u>Does your partner's reputation add value</u>? You should verify whether or not your partner firm has a good reputation. Do they deliver? Are their past clients raving fans or mumbling malcontents? What is their track record? Do your homework and ensure you are aligning yourself with reputable firms.

6. <u>Who will lead</u>? The last big area of friction can often be the question of who's in charge when it comes to the work or the client. You must work this out early. One common approach is to use the "best athlete" approach: whomever is best positioned or qualified with the client should lead, realizing this can change depending on the client and the work. This approach requires trust, however. If your relationship with your partner is strong, you'll have no problems. But it's worth thinking about.

The bottom line is if you cannot clearly and easily see the partnership making you better, in *every* respect, then stop. Look for another partner or go it alone. Do not rush, either. Take your time. Any agreements that are signed must be reviewed by your attorney. An ounce of prevention is worth a pound of cure.

Strive for Fairness for Lasting Partnerships

Dave (name changed) and I had been pursuing a new line of business over the past year. He owned a new technology for helicopter maintenance. It was amazing. It was relatively inexpensive but paid big dividends in lower maintenance costs, increased aircraft reliability and safety, and was already successfully in use by the Israeli military. He came to me asking that I assist him with breaking into the US market. We negotiated a revenue-sharing plan, and I was quite content with the whole arrangement. I was just happy to have this opportunity. In our agreed deal, he certainly stood to gain the most, but he had also invested the most, took the most risk, and owned the intellectual property. The deal made sense to me.

After some effort, we were on the verge of signing our very first large customer, with the potential to make our companies incredibly wealthy. Dave then came to see me and said, "We need to renegotiate our deal." I thought to myself, "Uh-oh. He wants a bigger cut." Right? Who wouldn't think that? But that's not what he did. He reduced his own portion to give me a larger portion of the revenue. Really? Who does that?

Dave, who was a successful real estate developer with properties in New York City, Dominican Republic, and other areas, was a brilliant businessman. He realized the value of developing and keeping good relations in a partnership or business deal. He had a business principle he'd learned over the years and to which he stuck religiously. It was this: a lasting and healthy partnership is better for all, and for a partnership to last, all parties have to be content that they are being treated fairly.

"A lasting and healthy partnership is better for all, and for a partnership to last, all parties have to be content that they are being treated fairly."

Dave said, "Wayland, I have been thinking that our original deal needed to change. I'm concerned that a year or two from now, you might feel like our deal isn't so good for you and perhaps regret that you did not negotiate a bigger share, and this would lead to you feeling mistreated and degrade our relationship. I want this relationship to last a very long time, and it's worth it to me and to our business that you always feel fairly treated. So, I'd like to reduce my portion and raise your portion."

I was flabbergasted. The portion increase he offered was very good for my firm. I began to see why he was such a successful developer in a business that relied heavily on partnerships and collaboration. He got it. I absolutely felt like our partnership was fair and that I was being treated properly. We went on to do well and years later are still good partners.

Just as a good marriage is the best thing ever invented in life, a bad marriage can be the worst thing ever invented. It's the same with partnerships. Its greatest strength—two firms working together on a common goal—is also its greatest weakness if you are not aligned well.

PRINCIPLE 1

A business partnership can be just like a marriage, either the best or worst thing ever invented in life. Take care who you choose. Strive to maintain fairness for a lasting partnership.

CHAPTER EIGHTEEN

When Doing Nothing Is the Winning Strategy

"Patience and perseverance have a magical effect before which difficulties disappear and obstacles vanish."

—John Quincy Adams

MY HIGH SCHOOL FOOTBALL team was in the dumps. We had just lost three consecutive games, and our season had just started. It can be very depressing for young teenage boys who've just put in long August practice sessions in the extreme heat, enduring injuries, aching muscles, not to mention the loss of our free time to have fun with our friends, and to now see the high school district standings with that glaring *0* staring at us under the *Wins* column. I began to ask myself, "Why am I putting myself through all of this? What's the point?"

"Well, if you guys would do your jobs, we would have a chance," Carl, who was the starting linebacker, yelled at us. He was right. We were making multiple mistakes, not executing well, forgetting our plays, losing our concentration, just not working together at all. There was lots of finger-pointing, name-calling, and enough blame to go around. But how bad was it, really? As I recall, it was pretty bad. Many would have advised us to do the "focus on the positives" strategy. But there weren't many positive things to say. We didn't score many points. Our kicker was missing field goals. We had trouble hanging on to the ball, losing it to the other team. I'm afraid that strategy would have been just as depressing as starting over.

Surprisingly, over the next three weeks, we would win all of our games. Suddenly, the criticisms and finger-pointing went away. All of the things we were doing badly seemed to disappear. All the criticisms that we were hurling at each other turned into praise and support. What a difference a few weeks made.

What had happened? Why were we doing better? What magical leadership or organizational strategy had been implemented? What self-help leadership book had the coach studied? No one cared, actually. We were winning, and nothing cures losing like winning. But, in my opinion, there was a reason for our success—and it was nothing.

The best thing that happened was *nothing*. Our coach felt the team was capable, our game plans were good, we had good players, we had what we needed to get the job done. So, he did nothing . . . that is, he didn't make any wholesale changes. We did go back and review the basics and practice those (blocking, tackling), refine and improve them—the things everyone is supposed to know and do all the time—but nothing really different or special. He encouraged us to keep working hard and improving individually, take responsibility for our own role on the team, and we would see success. He was right. When we were losing, there really was nothing wrong with our players, our strategy and plans, or our approach. The team just needed time to gel, to work with each other, and continue to improve individually. All we needed was more time, not a new plan.

Often in business, when things aren't working, we quickly try to jump in and "fix it." I have a particular weakness in this area. It's extremely hard for me to sit on my hands, to be patient, to give things time to mature and develop, to allow the strategy time to work. I want to jump in and fix it, to tinker with the plan, to swap out varying elements of the strategy, to keep trying new things. This can make things worse—much worse. Imagine if after only a couple days I keep digging up the seeds I've planted in my garden to see if they're growing fast enough. I'd never get the joy of watching them grow and then the pleasure of tasting fresh vegetables from my garden. Yes, I know that's a simple example, but it easily makes my point. When you start a new plan or project, it must be given time to germinate and grow, to see if it is actually going to work.

You might think, "But waiting feels like I'm doing nothing, leaving everything to chance." This is so not true. You are actively doing something—actively waiting. You're making a decision, you're doing something, you're allowing the plan to evolve. You've thought very hard and long about your plans. Now give them time to work. Don't abandon them too quickly.

So, before you go changing your game plan, firing/hiring people, implementing a new strategy, buying more equipment, going into debt, consider whether any action is required at all. You may have the right people, the right plan, the right client and market. It might just be that you need a little more time. Nothing may be wrong.

"Nothing may be wrong."

Encourage your team to always keep working and learning, improving in their individual skills and roles within your firm. Review your plans and strategies and make adjustments, if necessary. But don't fix something that's not broke. Often, in business and life, things move like a large cargo ship about to berth. The ship, for safety and control reasons, is moving very slowly as it approaches the pier. Any maneuvers that need to be made at this speed happen slowly. The captain may want to turn the vessel to the right, so he puts the rudder fully to the right. But guess what? Nothing happens immediately. It takes several minutes to turn the ship. If the captain starts throwing the rudder back and forth, making corrections because nothing is happening seconds afterward, he'd never make his destination. He must be patient. He makes a move with the rudder. He watches it for a minute. He makes another move. He watches it. In this way, he can calmly and with positive control make the ship go where he wants, safely.

If you find, after some time has gone by, that things aren't working as hoped in your business, be slow to make wholesale changes. Make a small move, then watch it. Make another move, then watch it. Allow time for your moves to be confirmed and for them to show results. Then consider your next move.

You may find that things start improving, that you start winning, and all those issues you saw previously have begun to disappear. As I said earlier, "Nothing cures losing like winning."

PRINCIPLE 2

Often, the best strategy during difficult times is to do nothing. Consider whether any action is required at all. Moving too quickly can make things worse. Don't fix something that isn't broken.

CHAPTER NINETEEN

Stop Doing What's Not Working—Duh!

"Sometimes the obvious answer isn't so obvious."

IN THE LAST CHAPTER, I made the point that we need to be careful before we take corrective actions in our businesses. Moving too quickly, without giving your plans or strategies a real chance to work, can do a tremendous amount of harm, waste valuable resources, and do nothing to improve your situation. In this chapter, I want to show you the value of a mentor, someone who can view your situation with fresh eyes and help you see what might be a blind spot in your thinking.

Around 2009, my small business had really hit troubled waters. After years of success—ten years, to be precise—something had changed. What used to come easily—clients, new opportunities, contract wins—was now incredibly difficult to obtain. Healthy profit margins had evaporated to margins so thin that any unexpected interruption in cashflow was a major problem. My credit line balances had started to creep up as I dipped into them to keep the business functioning. I was even considering laying off a couple of key senior employees because their salaries had grown so much over the years, deservedly so, but were now a real financial burden with the revenue shrinkage.

My personal life had also started to suffer. My wife and I were getting more short-tempered with each other. I'm sure it was more me than her. I was getting very worried, very nervous about the business. My mind was playing out depressing scenarios, and they all ended horribly. I had trouble seeing my situation positively. My stress levels were enormous. I am sure this resulted in me treating my sweet, loving soul mate in ways I'm ashamed of. Something I regret very much. I'm happy to report that our love for each other kept us firmly together, but that isn't to say we didn't struggle.

In addition, my children were observing, "What's wrong with Dad?" I had less and less time for them. I missed some of their school and other personal events. Why? I justified my actions by telling myself I was trying to keep a sinking ship afloat. I had over forty employees and felt a tremendous responsibility to them. They depended on the income from our company for their mortgage payments, their retirement funds, their financial goals, and the means to live their lives. I took this very, very seriously. Perhaps, too seriously? I focused completely on the business and put my family almost completely to the side—probably one of the worst things I could've done. I'm happy to report that, much like my loving wife, my children showed their true colors by loving and supporting me, and forgiving me, during this dreadful time. I don't deserve my kids. They're wonderful.

My business and life were out of sync, out of balance, and out of options. Something had to change. I sought out one of my mentors. He sat down with me and asked me to tell him what was going on. He listened to me rant for about thirty minutes before he held up his hand, signaling he had heard enough.

> ***"One of the greatest values of mentors is the ability to see ahead what others cannot see and to help them navigate a course to their destination."***
>
> **—John C. Maxwell**

"So, you've told me about the part of your business that is struggling. Is there another part that is doing well?" he asked. "Yes," I said and began to describe it. It was a smaller but still significant part of my business, and it was doing nicely. It always had done nicely. In fact, I told him I expected it to grow and why.

Then he hit me with one of the best pieces of advice I've ever received. "First, concerning your personal life," he said, "make everything right with your wife and family. They don't deserve to be treated harshly by you, no matter what you're going through." He then added, "Concerning your business, why not stop doing what's not working . . . and do more of what is working?" Wait, what? I was blown away! The simplicity of his advice felt cruel but obvious, even mind blowing. I knew the moment he said those words that they were the right words. The answer was right there in front of me, staring me in the face. I was so close to the trees, I couldn't see the forest.

He continued, "I'm not trying to offend you, and I know what I said seems so obvious and simple, but sometimes it's the obvious and simple that is so hard to see when you're in the middle of a struggle." He was right. I had allowed my circumstances to affect how I treated my family. Plus, I was too close to the business problem to see the obvious answer. I was so focused on keeping all aspects of my business alive that I missed the opportunity. I also thought to myself, "This is why it's good to have a real mentor."

I told him he had not offended me at all. In fact, he may have just saved me, my family, and my business from greater harm.

This is a good time to emphasize the value of a mentor—someone who cares about you, is deeply experienced in life and business, and is someone you absolutely trust to speak into your life. If you don't have a mentor or mentors, stop reading now and make a note in your journal or to-do list to get a mentor.

> ***"If you don't have a mentor or mentors, stop reading now and make a note in your journal or on your to-do list to get a mentor."***

I followed his advice. Over the next several months, I began the process of stopping what was not working. It was very hard. It involved laying off people that were in the "not working" part of the business, renegotiating leases, offloading equipment, and letting all my partners and clients in the affected areas of my business know that this part of my firm was coming to an end. Next, I took the resources that were now freed up from my downsizing actions and put some of them into the part of my business that was working. This was the more fun part of the process.

The whole downsizing effort was one of the most difficult things I've ever done in business, but the resulting impact on my business was worth it. We emerged smaller yet stronger and better positioned for growth into smarter areas of business. Since I made these changes, we've tripled in growth and have even more opportunities for further growth—opportunities that didn't previously exist until I made the strategic steps my mentor recommended.

Dr. Henry Cloud, in his book *Necessary Endings*, uses the illustration of pruning a rose bush to talk about how we sometimes have to cut back or end certain activity for the health of the entire organization. When growing a rose bush, you are required to prune it regularly to keep it as healthy and beautiful as possible. The three things you prune are (1) the obvious dead branches, (2) the sick or diseased branches, which seems fairly obvious, but the final thing you prune is not so obvious—(3) the branches or offshoots that are sucking life from the main part of the bush.

What you usually see is a nicely constructed main body of a bush, with one or two branches that stick out beyond the main body. These offshoots may seem healthy, but they are taking life away from the main body of the bush, and make the bush look quite odd instead nicely shaped. The only thing to do to keep the energy flowing to the main part of the bush and to maintain a well-shaped plant is to trim them back, which sometimes is hard because they can have such beautiful flowers on them. But if you don't do it, the main body of the bush suffers, and the resulting shape of the bush is compromised.

In the same way, our businesses have to be pruned from time to time. Anything that takes away from the main part of your business, your core services and offerings, needs to be eliminated to keep the main part of your business healthy. Like the rose bush illustration, some things are obvious and easy to prune back. However, like the healthy off-shoot, it can be difficult to prune when there may have been some good aspects to that part of the business in the past. But ask yourself, "Is this part of my business still working? Does it contribute to the core of my business?" If you can't answer yes to those questions, then it may be time to prune that branch in order to keep the main body of the bush healthy and beautiful.

PRINCIPLE 3

Stop doing what's not working, and do more of what is working. Prune those activities that do not contribute to your core business. Get a mentor to advise you.

CHAPTER TWENTY

Making Tough Employee Decisions

"You must do what's best for your organization and current employees. That must be the priority. But consider you may also be doing a big favor for the dismissed employee."

IF YOU STAY IN business long enough, you will face tough decisions. This is a fact. But of all the tough decisions you will face, none will be more challenging than those regarding your employees, especially a decision to end someone's job. These people have families, obligations, hopes, and dreams, and your decision to fire them or lay them off will have a detrimental effect on them. It can be a depressing and unfortunate situation, at least to me—and I hope for you, too. If you can easily and routinely terminate someone, check your pulse to see if you're still a warm, compassionate human being. This is a hard decision. It should be hard. I don't ever want it *not* to be hard. If it ever gets easy, I will worry about myself, and my humanity.

And because this is a tough decision, the temptation is to put it off—to delay the decision or even avoid it. This helps no one: not you, not the employee, not the organization. Chuck Swindoll once said, "The habit of always putting off an experience until you can afford it, or until the time is right, or until you know how to do it is one of the greatest burglars of joy. Be deliberate, but once you've made up your mind, jump in." I've seen managers delay these decisions, and they are miserable. When they finally do it, they are so relieved. If you've made your decision, why wait?

How Do I Know When to Dismiss an Employee?

It almost goes without saying that if this employee has a belligerent attitude, shows no willingness to change, or has committed an actual offense of any kind, you must take immediate steps to dismiss them. But assuming the conditions for obvious dismissal do not exist, you might be asking yourself how to know when it's time to terminate their employment? The answer is situationally dependent, but consider this: the fact that you are asking yourself this question might be a hint that you know the answer—the time may be now. Other indicators that it might be time are as follows:

1. After repeated counseling and performance reviews, the employee has not improved to an acceptable level. Moreover, even if this employee has shown a good attitude and willingness to improve, if the improvements do not materialize, you still must act.

2. The decrease in productivity is forcing other employees to do extra work beyond their regular duties, mostly carrying the employee in question. Not only is this costly, but this can also lead to feelings of resentment from the others, which can be very disruptive to the work environment.

How Do I Dismiss Them?

I am a *big* believer in personal, face-to-face meetings with the employee you intend to dismiss. I've seen employers dismiss employees with a letter, an email, a phone call—all of which I disagree with. Everyone deserves the respect and dignity of a personal, private, face-to-face delivery of the news. Sit down with them. Don't waste their time with idle chitchat. Get politely to the point and explain your decision. The meeting need not take long. Five or ten minutes would seem about right, assuming there are no issues to be discussed. I would suggest that if you believe the meeting will be difficult, ask another manager to join you as a witness and to offer support for your decision. I also think any real boss will do these kinds of tasks him or herself and not delegate this responsibility. Show some leadership; own the situation.

New Beginnings Often Start With an Ending

Also, consider this. Many times, I've dismissed someone and later learned that they found a better situation for themselves. If I hadn't dismissed them, they would not have improved their situation. For something new to begin, something else has to end. Endings are a part of life. I understand they will not appreciate this fact the day you dismiss them, but I tell you this for your encouragement. It's still a tough thing to do, but consider that you may be doing them the biggest favor by forcing them to reconsider their futures, get back out in the job market, and open up their lives to other opportunities.

It was time to let Dave (name changed) go. Dave had been with my small business for many, many years. He had been integral to our success. He had become a good and very loyal colleague. Dave was talented, dependable, and hardworking. We had grown close through work, but also through personal experiences. Our families spent time together, and we shared the joys and tragedies of life. We were good friends, indeed. How could I possibly consider letting him go?

Things had changed. Our market and clientele had changed, and our business had to change with it to stay viable and competitive—become leaner and more agile. Dave's salary was big—too big for our changing situation. In this new and emerging era of our business, we needed to evolve. If Dave had evolved with us, he would have been worth the higher salary. But he had not. Dave's legacy skill set was great under our original business model, but not now. I could no longer afford to carry him. In fact, I had carried him too long, delaying one of my toughest decisions as the owner. I did not want to have this conversation. I liked—maybe even loved—Dave. He had become like family. I probably delayed this decision by a year or more. That was a big mistake.

I did not fully appreciate the fact that by delaying this decision, I was harming both Dave and myself. I was doing a disservice to us both. When I began to realize that fact, I saw this inevitable discussion with Dave a little differently. For new beginnings to emerge, something else usually has to end. When a seed goes into the ground and dies, from it springs new growth, new possibilities. I saw this situation could be the beginnings of something new and better for Dave—something that fit better, paid better, and offered more satisfaction. But to start the new beginning, this situation had to end for Dave.

After viewing the situation as a natural part of life and considering that I could be opening new doors for Dave, I made up my mind and had the conversation. We said goodbye. It was hard. It was painful. And did things get better for us both after that? Not immediately. But things did get much better in time. In fact, Dave has a great position now with another firm, doing much better than he was with my firm. We freed up resources and brought in talent that better fit our business. We did much better afterward. It proved my point that by delaying this tough decision, I was hurting us both.

The lesson for me was to not delay the tough decisions. This isn't like fine wine where things improve with age—they can get worse. You must do what's best for your organization and all the current employees. That must be the priority. But I also believe you may be doing what's best for the dismissed employee.

Something had to end before something else good could emerge.

PRINCIPLE 4

Don't delay tough employee decisions. The welfare of the company and its current employees must come first. Plus, delays do yourself and the employee a great disservice.

CHAPTER TWENTY-ONE

When Not to Make a Big Decision

"When possible, it's almost always better to delay your big decisions until you are at your best."

DAVE (NAME CHANGED) WAS having one of those days. It started out with his alarm clock not waking him in time to make his early-morning meeting. He had forgotten to set the alarm. He forgot to pick up his laundry earlier, so he had almost nothing clean to wear, which made getting dressed a much harder and longer process than usual. His tube of toothpaste was empty since he hadn't had time to pick up another tube at the grocery store, which also meant he had no food in his pantry for breakfast. The first signs of anger began to develop.

As he was rushing to work, he hit a rather large object in the road and soon found himself with a flat tire. The roadside assistance service he paid for every month just happened to be extremely busy that hour due to the heavy rain pouring down, so it took over two hours for them to reach his car and assist with the repair. His clothes and hair were soaked, but he also had to stop for gas since his fuel gauge was on empty. His anger rose higher.

When he stepped out of his car in the office parking lot, his mobile phone fell from his pocket, shattering the screen. He'd just upgraded to a new phone two weeks ago. Now the phone's screen looked like a spider web of cracked glass. That phone cost him over $1,000, and he didn't opt for the insurance program at purchase, so now he was going to have to pay for the repairs. His anger was growing and had begun to compromise his objectivity.

As if he needed more stress, when he arrived at his office, Stanley was standing outside his door, asking to see him about an urgent matter concerning his pay and benefits, something he did quite regularly. Stanley had the unique talent of being able to make mountains out of small hills, to annoy at such levels of intensity that if this talent were an Olympic sport, he would undoubtedly have won the gold medal many times. After listening to Stanley rant, Dave's anger was now affecting his body; upset stomach, rapid heartbeat, sweaty brow, he was highly distracted and unable to focus mentally.

But the biggest problem was that Dave was about to step into a high-stakes meeting where he was expected to conduct a critical negotiation and give an indication of whether or not to commit his firm to a major project with huge corresponding amounts of risk and reward. What should Dave do?

HALT!

Making tough and important decisions is hard enough when you're feeling your best and everything is as it should be. But when you've had a day like Dave's, warning bells should be going off, saying, "Wait! This is not a good time to make a big decision!" Sometimes, after a stressful day like Dave's, I can still charge into an important decision because I'm blinded by my emotions and the desire to want to get things done, regardless of how I feel. Fortunately, I am usually halted by my colleagues and persuaded to slow down, seeing that I was not my usual self.

There are four times you should never make a big decision—and probably more, but without doubt these four should compel you to do whatever you can to delay your big decision, and to HALT!

1. Hungry. When you're hungry, medical science tells us that your body will not perform at its best, especially your brain. Deprived of the proper nutrition, not only will you be distracted, but your brain won't be operating at its best. You may get headaches and feel weak or lethargic. When I'm hungry, I can be very distracted. I can also feel lifeless, having no energy or drive. Even if you only grab a quick piece of fruit, put something in your stomach to eliminate the hunger.

2. Angry. When you're angry, your body can be affected in many ways that can inhibit your ability to think rationally, clearly, and with objectivity. You may miss some of the details that might be critical to your choices, and your emotions will most certainly filter any important information or advice, giving you an unhelpful bias in your judgment. If your anger is concerning a person, and they're involved in the big decision, that's even worse. If it's someone you can talk to and resolve whatever is angering you, then do it before you make your decisions. If it's someone that you cannot talk to, or may even be someone who is the object of the decision you're about to make, consider removing yourself from the decision. Or you could have someone you trust alongside that you can speak with frankly, someone you will listen to, that can give you their thoughts and observations as you deliberate. Don't trust yourself alone in these types of situations. Call on a friend. Don't let your anger lead you to the wrong decision.

3. Lonely. When you're lonely, you are susceptible to making choices that will somehow relieve you of your loneliness, rather than making decisions based on good analysis and judgment. When you're lonely, you will sometimes not see the full picture. You are just one person, with one brain and one perspective. You need other eyes, ears, and brains helping you. There is greater safety in numbers. Yes, it is true that you

alone will make the decision, but it doesn't mean that you alone can know it all or see it all. Let others help you gather all the information and related elements of the decision. Make your decision after you've done your best to look at the decision from many perspectives.

4. Tired. Many studies have been conducted on the effects of fatigue on the body and mind. Go to Google and search for it. The list is endless. I recently read that driving an automobile while sleep deprived is similar in risk to driving a car while drunk; your motor skills and decision-making ability are greatly compromised. Fatigue causes all kinds of problems. If you're tired, delay the decision until you are rested.

If you haven't noticed the acronym yet, it's *H* for hungry, *A* for angry, *L* for lonely, and *T* for tired—HALT. Next time you face an important personal or professional decision, pause and ask yourself if you're hungry, angry, lonely, or tired. If so, then HALT! When possible, it's almost always better to delay your big decisions until you are at your best. You also need a good team around you of friends or colleagues whom you trust and who can speak to you frankly and candidly about your state of mind. It is sometimes very hard to see things clearly yourself. Don't try to do life or business alone.

By the way, we can also make poor decisions even when we're at our best. I've been there, done that. But the risks are even greater when we're not at our best. Why increase the risk? Find a way to delay that big decision until you are ready. Give yourself the best chance for the best outcome.

PRINCIPLE 5

HALT! Delay the big decisions until you are at your best, not hungry, angry, lonely, or tired.

CHAPTER TWENTY-TWO

No Credibility, No Business

"Credibility is a leader's currency. With it, he or she is solvent; without it, he or she is bankrupt."

—John C. Maxwell

THERE'S NOTHING MORE PERSONALLY valuable than your credibility, because if you have it, then people trust you. If you do not have it and people feel they cannot trust you, you will struggle in almost every area of your business and your life. As John Maxwell says in the quote above, your credibility is your currency.

Merriam-Webster's dictionary defines *currency* as "the medium of exchange"—how business is transacted or how goods and services are exchanged. Without it, business becomes incredibly difficult. When two people or entities agree to do business, currency is how that business is realized. The currency could be dollars or other monetary medium like coins, it could be barter like the old country doctor who accepts eggs or cheese for his or her services, or most anything else as long as each party benefits. But without a form of currency or exchange, there can be no business transacted. Currency is essential.

Your credibility is your currency, or medium of exchange. If you have no credibility, then no business can be sustainably transacted.

There are always exceptions, of course, but they are few and unreliable. I admit I've done business with some who were not credible—holding my nose the entire time. I needed what they could provide, so I did business with them. If there had been any other choice, I would have taken it. I've only done this a couple times, and I was uncomfortable the whole time while doing business with them. As soon as I could, I cut ties, hoping never to do business with them again.

But generally, I will not do business with someone or some organization with no credibility. It's too risky, unpleasant, and can often bring credibility questions on you from others—sort of a guilt-by-association problem. As I've said before, if you stand too close to a mud puddle on a high traffic street, you risk getting splashed. Your reputation must be guarded carefully.

"Integrity is doing what you say;
honesty is saying what you do."

I challenge you to ask any successful entrepreneur about the importance of having credibility. I imagine you'll get many different answers, but they will most certainly involve trust. If you cannot trust the person you are about to do business with because they have no credibility, a successful relationship will be hard to achieve. Another word that will come up is *honesty*. In fact, honesty, integrity, and credibility are all synonymous. One way I like to think about honesty and integrity is to compare and contrast them like this: integrity is doing what you say; honesty is saying what you do. A business person of integrity will do what they said they would do, *and* they will accurately say what they have done, when it's all over, without embellishment. Think about it.

How does one become credible? Credibility has to be earned, much like respect. One can be given authority by an organization or person, much like a prime minister or president appoints someone to a position within their government. That person will be recognized as a person of authority. But that doesn't mean people will respect that person. The appointed person has to earn the respect of those with whom they work. An Army soldier will salute a senior officer in uniform, recognizing their position of authority without even knowing them personally. But that same soldier can only respect that senior officer if they have observed them conduct themselves over time in such a way as to earn that soldier's respect.

To gain the respect of business associates around you, your clients, as well as your employees takes time. Everyone must see how you conduct yourself in various situations: under pressure, when fatigued, making more good choices than wrong ones, sensing your pure motivations or honest purpose, your priorities. Are you selfless or selfish? Do you have integrity and honesty as I've described them above? When you've earned the respect of those around you, your credibility is established. Below are a few tips to help you establish and maintain your credibility. Guard your credibility as you would guard anything of great value: protect it, cultivate it, and cherish it.

Tips to Establish & Grow Your Credibility

1. Be accurate. This is critical in your daily communications and interactions with people in all areas of your life, personal and professional. To the best of your ability, ensure what you are saying or writing is accurate. Check your facts. If you're not sure, then caveat your statements with something like this: "I've been unable to confirm this information, but it's the best information I have right now." This is not the time to be creative or clairvoyant. Be real, factual, and objective. There will be the temptation to say something, anything, so you look like you're knowledgeable or informed. Don't take the bait.

2. Quickly correct errors. When you learn that something you truly believed was correct is not, quickly tell everyone.

Apologize. Retract your statement. People do not expect perfection, but they treasure honesty and intent. If they know you were giving them what you believed to be true, they will forgive the occasional error. It also increases your credibility when you are quick to correct the error. Remember, errors in information are not like fine wine—like bad news, they do not get better with age. Own it and quickly correct known errors. This is not a sign of weakness. If you try to hide or cover it up, and then it's later discovered, it will be much worse than if you'd just quickly corrected the error.

3. Reference your information. Tell everyone where you found it, or who said it, or what you directly observed. No one expects you to know it all. Knowing where the information came from puts a qualitative value on it, and people like that. Your credibility will grow.

4. Say, "I don't know." This is a legitimate answer to any question. Often we feel compelled or tempted to want to give an answer to a client or friend's question so much that we make up the information so as to be seen as an expert or knowledgeable. Big mistake. This will come back to haunt you and destroy your credibility. If you don't know the answer, say that clearly. You can then offer your opinion, or even speculate, but tell them that's exactly what you're doing. Don't appear to be stating facts when you don't know the facts.

5. Don't embellish. It's also tempting when you know a few facts to add your own facts. This again stems from wanting to appear to be an expert. It's okay to say, "Here's what I know," and tell them. Then you can go on to offer your opinion or speculate, but tell them when you're giving your opinion or speculating.

Credibility Advice: When It All Goes Wrong, Go Ugly Early!

In addition to my tips above, one more piece of credibility advice merits its own section in this chapter because it's that important: go ugly early!

When I was a teenager, I got three traffic tickets in *one day*, all at the same time! I was sixteen years old with a brand-new driver's license. This was the most tragic day of my life. I was cited for (1) riding a motorcycle with no helmet in a speed zone that was forty miles per hour or higher (the law in Logan, Utah, at the time), (2) I had run a stop sign in a hurry to get home for another commitment, and (3) I did not have my driving license on me, earning me three separate tickets. I felt like everything in my life was going totally wrong. I knew that when my father learned of this disaster, not only would I be the recipient of a crushing verbal tongue lashing, but every privilege I enjoyed in the world would be taken from me. Life as I knew it was about to end.

But wait! What if I just didn't tell him? What if I just hid the tickets or burned them? How would he know? I could watch the mail and make sure any notices received from the authorities would be filtered out and tossed. I could earn money and pay the fines. Yes, this could work, right? But then I remembered the insurance bill. I learned in driver's education classes that the authorities would eventually report any traffic incidents to some central database, and my insurance company would learn of it and adjust my father's bill upward. He would of course call them and inquire into the increase, and they would dutifully inform him of his felonious son and his crimes against humanity.

To my credit, I decided to "go ugly early" and tell him immediately what had happened. Yes, it was tough for a time, and I did pay for my crimes, but my father also congratulated me for coming clean and owning my mistakes. He added that had I waited, it would have been far worse for me. My interpretation of that statement was "Go ugly early!"

Like most folks, I have continued to make errors throughout my life—some of them real whoppers—and I have always remembered this lesson on coming clean sooner than later. This principle has served me well throughout my career where the stakes have been much larger in scope and scale, impacting many more lives beyond my own. Each time, whether it was a mistake with a client or, more critically, with my wife or family, by "going ugly early," problems have been more easily resolved and relationships maintained, sometimes even strengthened.

People know that no one is perfect. Human error is a part of life. But what people don't tolerate is hiding the truth, cover-ups, and deceit. They prefer to deal with an honest person, company, or firm, even if imperfect, and will respect you more after you've committed the error if you handle it properly. But not being responsible or accountable will usually cost you dearly, to say nothing of the damage to your own self-respect. No one will want to do business with you.

PRINCIPLE 6

Establish and maintain your credibility. Guard it at all times. As King Solomon the wise once said, "A good name is rather to be had than great riches."

CHAPTER TWENTY-THREE

Mitigating Financial Risk as a Startup

"You won't be able to eliminate the risks, but you can limit them."

HAVING A STARTUP BUSINESS can be the thrill of your professional life. How cool is it to make something out of nothing, to create something that did not exist before? Then to experience the excitement that comes when that creation comes alive, grows, and provides you with a respectable income. There's no feeling like it on earth, in my opinion.

If you want to start your own business, of course you need a product or service and a customer willing to pay you for it. Beyond that, however, you need to invest time thinking about risk and how to manage it. I mean, how do you know your startup will succeed? You don't. Who will pay money for your idea? Will your startup be sustainable over the long term? There are loads of questions you must answer. But perhaps one of the most significant risks is how you will fund it. There are many ways to approach funding your startup, and each comes with specific risks. You won't be able to eliminate the risks, but you can limit them.

Here are my suggestions to limit the risks in funding your startup:

1. Do your homework. Learn all you can about your prospective business, its market, potential customers, trends, conservative revenue and cost estimates, competitors—everything you can. Do thorough research. Talk to people in the business. Get and use a mentor experienced in your area of interest. Please don't skip this homework step and jump into the next steps. This step will inform your decisions and lay the foundation, increasing your chances of success.

2. Use what you've already got. I've been told that when you go to a casino to gamble, only take the amount of money you can afford to lose. I think that's excellent advice for a startup business. Use your own money, and just use what you can afford to lose. If you do this and everything goes bust in your startup, you'll be upset but not broke. You'll also be wiser and perhaps better prepared should you decide to take a second stab at it.

   Use your own tools, computers, vehicles, and other equipment at first. Later, when the revenue picture is much healthier, begin acquiring what you need. But again, make sure you need it. Also, think carefully about leasing versus owning your equipment. There are many good financial and business reasons to lease. Talk to your accountant.

   Leverage affordable and widely available services and technologies. These days you can get robust IT solutions for free or for minimal cost. You can also get various kinds of other services at a very low price. For example, you may not want to hire a full-time employee as your assistant when you can get essentially the same services virtually, on an as-needed basis, from many third-party providers.

   Call in favors from friends and family. If you need the

help, your friends and family might be willing to help you at no charge because they care about you. Nothing wrong with asking for some startup support from your personal network. I wouldn't abuse this, but it can help you get started.

3. Conserve your cash—cash is king. Don't buy anything for your startup until you need it. If you do need it, don't hesitate to buy it. But make sure you need it. And be sure not to confuse needs with wants.

   Ask your suppliers to give you favorable credit or payment terms. For example, ask them if they'll accept a "you get paid when I get paid" arrangement. When you get paid by your client, use that money to pay your suppliers, rather than using credit to pay them while you wait to be paid. This action will conserve your startup cash.

   If you need to hire direct labor (these are people you can invoice your client for), don't hire them as employees at first. Consider using them as independent contractors. Make sure they agree to the same conditions as your other suppliers; they get paid when you get paid, and they must provide their own health insurance, invoice you monthly, and manage their own taxes. But this can help you by conserving your cash and lowering your overhead. This strategy is usually meant to be temporary, best suited for the first year. If things really get going and longer-term business is assured, then you should take steps to bring everyone on as employees. But this is a great cash-management strategy for the startup phase of your business. This can be a great strategy for the long term, too, but make sure you understand the IRS rules on the use of independent contractors versus employees.

   Barter for products and services you might need. Offer to do something for a friend in exchange for the things you need. Sell off your unused personal stuff on eBay. You've probably got lots of things you don't want or use. Sell it and use the cash for your startup.

Don't quit your job until you know you've got the resources to keep your startup properly funded for the long term. This usually means long hours for you, and you'll probably have to be very creative in how you manage your time. This should only be a temporary solution, just until your startup can support you. Yes, this will mean long hours and an imbalance between your business and life, but most would consider it a justifiable sacrifice. Again, this is only temporary and is meant to conserve cash and avoid debt.

4. Use credit sparingly, as a last resort. After careful consideration, if you decide to use debt to help finance your startup, use low- or no-interest credit lines or credit cards. Pay these off as soon as possible. You could also consider personal loans from friends and family instead of a bank or lending company. If things go wrong, your friends will likely give you more time and better treatment than a bank. You can also borrow from your own savings, but remember to pay yourself back, with interest.

   The only kind of credit I like is credit used to help generate income. For example, if I get a contract from a client, I might need some equipment or other services to start work. Borrowing on a short-term basis to fund the contract start is a good use of credit. Using credit to buy a new desk or office decorations doesn't really directly help you generate income. You could get a desk at a thrift store, or perhaps you know someone who wants to get rid of their old desk for free, and you can decorate your office later or find a way to decorate with things you already own. Again, consider debt only as a last resort. Make sure you are only getting what you need, not what you want.

The main message of this chapter is to only use those resources you can afford to lose, if things go really wrong. You don't want to be left with serious financial troubles. Carefully consider the risks and put strategies in place to mitigate them. Many entrepreneurs don't get it right the first time but because they managed the risks were able to live to fight again another day and go on to succeed in their next attempt. But if they'd totally mismanaged the risks, they'd have been left in such a financial pit that another attempt would have been out of the question.

PRINCIPLE 7

Mitigate the risk to your startup business with strategies to conserve your cash and limit your financial exposure should things go wrong.

CHAPTER TWENTY-FOUR

A New Product or Service Offering

There is a big difference between taking a calculated risk and gambling with your business.

ONE OF THE THINGS I love as an entrepreneur is the excitement of doing new things—creating a new product offering, a new service, working with new partners, pursuing new customers. I enjoy the freedom. Whatever my mind can conceive, I can potentially achieve. I love that there is a whole world of possibilities out there. However, this freedom comes with risk. Not everything you think of should be pursued. There has to be a fair amount of due diligence performed. One must take care to ensure a proper balance between risk and reward.

So, you've got a new business and things are going well, but you now want to expand your business offerings—a new product or service. What are some of the things that need to be considered before jumping into a new business venture? Let me suggest several things. This following list is by no means comprehensive or exhaustive, nor is it in any particular order. Each person's situation will be different. So please take my list and add your own elements to it.

Questions to Consider Before You Venture Out

1. Is it complementary? Does this new venture offer something completely new or is it related to your current business offerings? Offering a new product or service that complements what you already provide makes much more sense than starting something completely new for which you have little or no expertise, corporate knowledge, customer base, or talent. That is not to say that offering something entirely new is out of the question, only that it brings greater risk than a complementary offering. Your current customers, a great place to sell your new offering, will be more likely to consider a complementary offering than an entirely new offering.

   An example of a new complementary offering would be to offer consulting services to complement the software you already sell. Or if you sell fitness equipment, you may want to offer online video training exercises. These are complementary offerings. It wouldn't be a tremendous leap for your client to consider. It may even drive more fitness equipment sales. However, if you sell fitness equipment and you're considering offering gardening supplies and equipment, your current clients would be much less likely to consider this over the training videos. This might even confuse your clients, originally thinking of your company as a health and fitness rather than a gardening firm. These would not be complementary offerings.

2. What are your assumptions? What you assume may make or break the entire new venture decision. Are your assumptions realistic? Are your estimates about customer demand, potential revenue, talent availability, and startup costs all realistic or overly optimistic? Be conservative in your estimates, then add another 25 percent for error or the unexpected. Is it affordable? Ask a close friend or associate for their honest feedback on

your assumptions. Make sure your assumptions are *not* biased in favor of your new venture but are objective and truthful. I've made the mistake of not vetting my assumptions with trusted allies, leading me to make a biased decision. We can very easily tell ourselves what we want to hear. When you want something badly, your bias is hard to control. That's why you need another perspective. Biased assumptions could lead to disastrous outcomes.

3. What are the risks? The real question here is whether you can afford to lose the entire venture's investment if it goes bust and safely continue to operate. You do not want to put the whole of your current business at risk if the new venture doesn't work. Please understand I'm not saying to avoid all risk. As entrepreneurs, risk is part of our world, and we thrive in it. We love it. But there is a big difference between taking a calculated risk and gambling with your business. Don't gamble. Know and mitigate the risks.

   One sound strategy to ensure you understand the risk is to do a business wargame with your staff, employees, or trusted business associates. I'm not talking about a large and expensive, time-consuming process. Keep it simple. Set aside a few hours. Bring everyone in and brief them on your idea, as objectively as possible, not trying to overly sell them or bias them on the idea. Show them not only the good side but also the bad side or risks involved. Be honest. Now open the floor and ask them to be critical, even brutal, regarding the idea. Walk through different scenarios that you could face—stiff competition, economic recession, low demand, and so on. How would you respond in each scenario? If you do this right, you'll end the wargame with greater insights and honest feedback on the idea. You are much better prepared to consider the risk.

4. Is this a passion? Ask yourself, why do you want to do this? What is driving you? Sure, there are the financial benefits, and I'm not discounting them. But my experience with both successful and failed ventures has been that when I was more passionate about the venture, I was more successful. When I believed in the venture, that it would help people or organizations I care about, I was more committed. You need to be "all in," as they say in poker. If you and your team are not completely passionate and committed to this venture, it will show in your planning, communications, leadership, and results. So know why you want to do this.

These are just a few questions you need to consider before deciding on that new venture. Yes, there are other things, like your competitors, the local economy, regulatory requirements, investors, but the list above should lay the foundation for all the other factors you must consider.

PRINCIPLE 8

When considering a new offering, there is a big difference between taking a calculated risk and gambling with your business. Don't gamble.

Part Three Recap: Hard-Won Business Lessons That Work

PRINCIPLE 1

A business partnership can be just like a marriage, either the best or worst thing ever invented in life. Take care who you choose. Strive to maintain fairness for a lasting partnership.

PRINCIPLE 2

Often, the best strategy during difficult times is to do nothing. Consider whether any action is required at all. Moving too quickly can make things worse. Don't fix something that isn't broken.

PRINCIPLE 3

Stop doing what's not working, and do more of what is working. Prune those activities that do not contribute to your core business. Get a mentor to advise you.

PRINCIPLE 4

Don't delay tough employee decisions. The welfare of the company and its current employees must come first. Plus, delays do yourself and the employee a great disservice.

PRINCIPLE 5

HALT! Delay the big decisions until you are at your best, not hungry, angry, lonely, or tired.

PRINCIPLE 6

Establish and maintain your credibility. Guard it at all times. As King Solomon the wise once said, "A good name is rather to be had than great riches."

PRINCIPLE 7

Mitigate the risk to your startup business with strategies to conserve your cash and limit your financial exposure should things go wrong.

PRINCIPLE 8

When considering a new offering, there is a big difference between taking a calculated risk and gambling with your business. Don't gamble.

PART FOUR:

HARD-WON LIFE LESSONS THAT WORK

CHAPTER TWENTY-FIVE

Living Agreeable in a Disagreeable World

"When given the choice between being right or being kind, choose kind."

—Dr. Wayne W. Dyer

ONE OF THE MOST important skills a good leader will ever develop is his or her ability to handle conflict in the workplace—or anywhere else, for that matter. And perhaps the most difficult kinds of conflict to manage are those involving disagreements. It could be disagreements over policy, direction, decisions—most anything. Not handled properly, disagreements can become a festering wound that grows into something with a far-reaching negative impact throughout your organization, not to mention your personal life.

Just look at the world we live in now. I've never seen our national and global dialogue so emotionally charged with anger and hatred. We've not acquitted ourselves very well, like mature leaders and adults. Our children are not properly shown how to handle friction or conflict with others. I'm unhappy with all sides politically, culturally, and socially. This has not been our proudest moment in time as a civilized people.

"The goal should be to find a way to resolve differences and move forward, for the good of everyone— not to win the argument."

I will not point fingers since that's unhelpful and many others are already doing this. However, I would like to offer my thoughts on what I think we should do to better conduct ourselves and manage disagreements, both in the workplace and in life. No, I don't believe my suggestions will solve all problems, but I hope to get some people thinking before they say or act in such a way as to inflame their disagreements. The goal should be to find a way to resolve differences and move forward, for the good of everyone—*not* to win the argument.

Thoughts on Living Agreeable

1. First, accept that it is okay to agree to disagree and realize that you can do this and still be friends. Just think of that! I can disagree with you, on anything, and still be your friend. Wow! We can even go to a restaurant together and enjoy an evening out. For example, I saw United States senators Orrin Hatch and Ted Kennedy do this, and there were never two more politically opposite people in the world. They agreed on very little politically, but at the end of the day, they always remained friends. They weren't perfect, but overall they kept things professional, not always resorting to personal attacks. Their debates on the Senate floor were legendary, but so was their friendship. They were a bit of an odd couple, but a great example of how you can agree to disagree with someone and still be good friends. The real miracles were the times they joined forces to pass important legislation, which we benefit from today. They were both great statesmen.

2. Accept that if someone disagrees with you, they are *not* a bad person, just different. Keep the issue and the person separate.

When you get personal and start name-calling, for example, it's *very* hard to achieve anything helpful or sustainable going forward. Differences should be a strength in any family or organization, not a place to draw battle lines. If someone disagrees with you, it doesn't mean they are the enemy. Don't fall into that trap.

3. Consider for a moment that your position might be wrong. I know, I know—but it is possible. You must stay open minded. As Matt Keller says in his book *The Key to Everything*, staying teachable is critical to everything in your life. When you think you know it all, you've just taken away any further chance to grow or learn. When you are considering an issue that is gridlocked in disagreement, beware of confirmation bias—the tendency to interpret new evidence as confirmation of one's existing beliefs or theories. How can you avoid confirmation bias? Ask yourself, "Am I listening to affirm or to inform?" If it's to affirm, then you aren't listening. Your mind is closed. Stay committed to lifelong learning.

4. When you lose your cool, you lose your ability to make good decisions. Shayne Hughes, in his book *Ego Free Leadership*, said, "Ineffective communication always leads to making the wrong decision. When smart people don't listen to each other, their value cancels each other out." Have you ever seen anyone make a really poor decision while they're upset? Yep, me too. As mentioned earlier in this book, I use the HALT acronym as a mental check on my decision-making; never make a big decision when you're hungry, angry, lonely, or tired—HALT.

5. People who are peacemakers and peace-maintainers attract others who are looking for leadership, progress, and a healthy work environment. Be that leader. When you respond harshly, you lose your credibility and appear weak, out of control, and

undisciplined. You lose the respect of your employees and coworkers, not to mention your family and friends. In stressful and tense situations, I've always respected my bosses who kept their cool more than those who completely lost it.

6. Accept that "compromise" is *not* a dirty word. It does *not* show weakness. It's a proven way to live. Look at any healthy, long-lasting marriage. Without compromise, that marriage could not last—ask them. I've been married forty-two years, and without the ability to compromise, my marriage would have ended long ago. And remember, a good compromise is when all parties are equally unhappy or happy. If one side has taken advantage of the other, the agreement won't last, and it was not a good compromise. The attitude of "my way or the highway" is a quick path to gridlock, waste, inefficiency, failure, and unhappiness. Nothing will work.

"And by the way, it's not about you. If it is, then none of what I'm saying in this chapter will make any sense."

7. Consider you don't always have to be right. Peace is worth almost any price. When given the choice between being right or being kind, be kind. Rarely will a harsh response result in anything positive. It only makes you feel better temporarily. And by the way, it's not about you. If it is, then none of what I'm saying in this chapter will make any sense.

8. When you get offended—and you will get offended—make the decision to let it go. Be first to be the magnanimous one. William James once said, "The secret of wisdom is knowing what to overlook." You have to learn to let it go! Some things are just not worth the fight. Keep the main thing the main thing. Keep the mission or goal in mind.

What's the Ultimate Goal?

Some people will say, "Yes, Wayland, these are all good things to consider, but sometimes the issues are so critical that I think it's okay to respond emotionally, to make the point, to hold firm in my position, to appear disagreeable, to move my agenda along. I can't show weakness." My response would be "What is your ultimate goal? To destroy the relationship, enter gridlock, and fail? Or is the goal to find a way forward for the good of everyone, and to succeed?"

If the goal is to find a solution, then that almost always means compromise when disagreements are encountered. And the only way to reach a compromise is through thoughtful and respectful dialogue and to be willing to give in order to gain a balanced, sustainable agreement.

Choose to be kind—be agreeable—and win for everyone!

PRINCIPLE 1

In a conflict, the goal should be to find a way to resolve differences and move forward, for the good of everyone—*not* to win the argument.

CHAPTER TWENTY-SIX

Cultivate Your Close Relationships

"A beautiful and productive garden cannot be left to itself; it must be cultivated."

WITHIN YOUR SUPPORT SYSTEM of relationships, there is usually one person who is closest to you, means more to you, has your permission to speak into your life more than any other, whose opinion matters more than any other. This is usually someone you have strong feelings for, someone you possibly are in love with, are vulnerable with, and who brings joy to your life. For many entrepreneurs, that special person is usually your spouse or girlfriend or boyfriend, but may be a parent or guardian, sibling, or mentor. You know who they are.

To be able to operate at your best and highest, those life-giving relationships need to be strong, happy, and at peace. When they are not, it has numerous negative consequences—at the very least, the tremendous distraction it causes, and at the most, the effect it could have on your health. That special someone in my life is my wife of forty-two years, Karen. When our relationship is under duress, I struggle to get anything accomplished outside of the normal daily routine. Nothing really significant or important is easy to do. My focus is compromised, and my ability to think creatively, to innovate, to be my best is also compromised. My stomach is in knots, I stop eating—in fact, I stop nearly every healthy thing I should be doing, reaching for comfort food, become a couch potato, and so forth. Oh yes, I completely go into a fetal position, both mentally and physically.

It seems funny to realize that one of the very best things any of us can have is a special, close relationship with someone special that we love. We can feel strong, empowered, creative, and motivated to conquer the world. Yet that very same relationship can also be the worst thing for us if that relationship is in great distress. However, we should not hesitate to choose to have a loving relationship out of fear of it going wrong. The upside far outweighs the downside. What we can do is take steps to ensure our relationships stay strong, healthy, and sustainable. How can we do this? I offer you my thoughts below.

1. <u>Keep your priorities properly set</u>. Special people are critical to you and your dreams and should come first; that means before anything else in your life. If you've allowed your priorities to get out of order, then take the time to correct or rebalance them. Tell those special people you're sorry, do something to show them you're sorry, and determine within yourself to prevent that from happening again. If it does happen again, don't quit trying; just hit the reset button and start again. No one expects perfection from you, especially those who really love and care for you. But they should expect to see a willingness to admit wrongdoings, apologize, and correct the errors.

   If you've allowed your business to take precedence over your loved ones, you've made a mistake. Admit it to them. Apologize for it, saying specifically where you've failed. Express your love to them and tell them your intentions to prevent a reoccurrence. An attitude of humility and love will enable you to make course corrections when you fail and to keep those most important relationships. Don't let your pride keep you from admitting you were wrong and risking the loss of the most important people in your life. Be an adult. Admit the fault. Take your punishment. Show your love.

My experience has shown that my wife's love for me grows even bigger when we are vulnerable and humble ourselves with each other, admitting our faults and expressing our love. We have survived some horrific challenges, always emerging stronger and more in love. If you do this, regardless of the challenges that will come your way, you will see your relationships thrive.

2. Proactively plan time for the special people in your life. We can easily get overcome by daily events, making busyness our business—losing sight of what really matters. Make time for the special people in your life. Be intentional. When you sit down to plan your work, whether you do it daily, weekly, or monthly, include your personal life and time with those special people in your life. Many people use the dinner hour as a sacred time with family. Some use sports. Others plan times on the weekends or special holidays. Whatever you can do, plan it, and put it on your calendar. Then, when you are with them, be with them.

   What do I mean? Put your phone down. Take the headphones off. Turn off the television. Remove any distractions. Be with your family or friends—focus on them. Show them they are the most important thing. Once, when my daughter, Lynnsey, saw me silence my phone and put it away, she smiled at me and said, "Wow." That's all she had to say. I knew she was thinking, "Wow, Dad is focusing totally on me." It's a great gift you can give your loved ones—the gift of you.

It's a great gift you can give your loved ones—the gift of you.

3. Periodically check in with these special people. Just as you would with your employees or customers, seek feedback from those closest to you. Ask them how they feel about your relationship—would they give it high marks? Be honest and sincere when you do this. Also, be prepared for any answer. You might be surprised. If they really care about you, they will give possibly some of the most valuable information you will ever receive. Open your mind. Put your feelings into neutral. Use this feedback.

   For example, during a feedback session with my son Nick, I heard some very difficult things from him about how I treated him, how I made him feel, and why he felt that way. I was very uncomfortable, sad, and disappointed—in me. I'm ashamed to admit I didn't respond well at first. I was defensive, trying to explain my behavior. But eventually I had to own it. Regardless of what I did or didn't do, I was hearing how he felt. I made it a point to shut up and listen, not start thinking of how to respond when he was talking. That was the most important thing.

   We had a serious discussion about it all. I apologized. He apologized. I said what I would try to do better in the future, as did he. We had to talk more in coming days because we were still not doing the best, but things slowly got better. I'm happy to say that today my relationship with him is better than ever. We still have the occasional disagreement, but we respond much better now than we used to. It's a win for us. I love my son. That drives everything. I am determined my own intentions will give way to my love for him. Our relationship is the most important thing. These discussions with Nick also caused me to examine my behavior with others in my family and at work. I asked myself, "Am I like this with them, too?" The answer was sometimes yes. So, as a result of my difficult but honest discussions with Nick,

I became more aware of myself and improved the way I interacted with others. A good result all the way around.

Just like a beautiful and productive garden cannot be left alone, you must also take care of your relationships. If you plant good seed, pull weeds, till the soil, water the plants, you will enjoy the wonderful results, both in your business and your life. Neglect your garden and it will not be beautiful or productive, but only a problem.

PRINCIPLE 2

To be able to operate at your best and highest, your life-giving relationships need to be strong, happy, and healthy. Make them your highest priority.

CHAPTER TWENTY-SEVEN

Disentangle Your Mind to Ease Worries

"Worry does not empty tomorrow of its sorrow, it empties today of its strength."

—Corrie ten Boom

CORNELIA "CORRIE" TEN BOOM was a Dutch watchmaker and Christian who, along with her father and other family members, helped many Jews escape the Nazi Holocaust during World War II. She was imprisoned for her actions. Her story has inspired generations of people. No, I won't tell you her story. You'll have to read it for yourself in her book, *The Hiding Place.* I highly recommend it for inspirational as well as historical significance reasons.

Corrie has said so many wonderful things and is frequently quoted in a variety of mediums by many authors and public speakers. My favorite Corrie quote regarding the subject of worry is "Worry does not empty tomorrow of its sorrow. It empties today of its strength."

As a small business owner or entrepreneur, your situation can usually best be described by the old axiom "The buck stops here." Everything rests on your shoulders. You're the CEO, the bookkeeper, payroll clerk, client manager, customer service representative, business developer, human resources manager, secretary, and doorman! You wear many, many hats because, well, that's what you do; it's what you have to do. You've generally got more time than money, which means you step up and get things done on your own to conserve scarce resources.

This way of business life can lead to high stress, sleepless nights . . . and lots and lots of *worry*! Unfortunately, this is normal for most small business owners and entrepreneurs. I worried so much that I often didn't even realize how much I was worrying, how big of a load I was carrying, until things slowed down and I had a chance to notice it or think about it. Then I'd get depressed and feel very tired. I didn't know what to do about it. So I just kept pushing.

But step back with me for a moment. Ask yourself this question, in all honesty: "What good am I doing by worrying? Is it solving anything? Am I getting anything done? Am I getting better revenues? Am I lowering my costs? Am I improving employee morale? How about my personal life; is worrying improving my relationships? Is it improving my quality of life?" I can confidently say that your answer will be a resounding "NO!" because that was my answer, too!

Worry is like paying interest on money you haven't even borrowed and makes about as much sense when you really think about it. Let's say a big event is coming up, in your life or business. It's the responsible thing to consider this event, weigh potential outcomes, assess your ability to manage or respond to it, and make plans to respond. But what we often find ourselves doing is going beyond just considering this event to obsessing over it. There's a big difference between considering something and obsessing over it. When this event starts to consume every idle thought, invade your rest or sleep time, lower your coping ability, distract you from other important people and matters in your life—you're now obsessing, paying interest on money you haven't borrowed. Think about it. Nothing has happened, but you're acting as if it has.

You might be thinking, "Yes, Wayland, but isn't it good to closely examine these things to make sure you've got every potential outcome covered?" Yes, I do think that's important. But when you've considered everything, set the issue aside. Do something else. Fix dinner for your family. Go for a run or walk. Watch a good movie or sporting event. Read a really interesting book, not related to the subject of your worry. Play with your children. Listen to music. Paint a picture. Shift gears completely away from the event.

If you read Corrie's quote again, what is she really saying? Worry doesn't change the future one bit, but it does steal your energy—energy that could be used to tackle other problems or to enjoy the rest of your life. It's a waste. We've got to try to stop it! "Just like that, Wayland?" you ask. It might be just that simple. I believe we have the power to make the decision to change our thinking. It takes repetition and practice, but yes, we can do it. We can reprogram. I did it, and if I can do it, I know for certain you can. So I sat down and thought about what steps I would take to get myself off the worry and into a frame of mind more enjoyable and healthy.

Disentangle Your Mind and Stop Worrying

I'm a big believer in writing things down or journaling. I'm not talking about a planner only, but a blank notebook you set up to facilitate and organize your thoughts. What kind of thoughts? All kinds of thoughts. For example, I start every morning with a quiet hour for myself. Yes, that's a lot of time, so I get up very early depending on my schedule for the day. I use this hour to meditate, journal, and plan. You may want to try a half hour. You decide.

I begin by writing down three things I'm grateful for. It can be anything—good weather, the love of my spouse, food to eat, or a healthy body. Not only does this get your day started with a mindset of gratefulness, but it also gets the writing juices flowing. Then I think about how I feel at that moment. Am I stressed? Tired? Does my body ache? How do I physically feel? What is on my mind? What's bothering me? What am I happy about? What's going well? I write all this down. I also write out prayers and creative thoughts that come. Sometimes, right in the middle of this process, an invading thought will pop up, like "Gosh! I can't forget to pick up my prescription at the drugstore," or "I've got to get my dry cleaning before I go on my trip." When this happens, I pause and write down these administrative thoughts in a place in my notebook I can refer to later. When I do this, I can rest assured that the thought has been captured. I won't forget it, so now I find I can go back to my hour of meditation and planning. That interrupting thought is now off my radar.

This is your time to slow down and meditate. And when I say meditate, I'm not talking about sitting cross-legged with your legs under you and humming a mantra, but you can do that if that helps you—I'm all for it. I'm talking about thinking deeply and carefully, chewing on something mentally, quieting your mind and allowing thoughts to emerge. So, to make this easier to do and understand, I've listed the steps I follow below. Use and adjust them to make your time as helpful as possible.

1. First, write down everything in your journal that you're worried about, in detail. This is a regurgitation of everything that comes to mind. Get it all down on paper. No limits.

2. Then, annotate each item on your list as something you can or can't do something about. For example, if the first item listed that you are worrying about is "economic recession," you might write a *CD* next to it, which means you "can't do" anything about it. You can't control the national economy. If the second item listed is "unexpected cash shortages," then you might annotate a *C* next to it for "can do" something about it. Continue this process until each item on your list is categorized.

3. Go to a new clean page and write at the top *CAN'T-DO ITEMS.* Then transfer from your first list those items you labeled *CD,* leaving a few lines between each item for future notes. If there's nothing you can do about it, and it's something out of your control, then we are going to "park" that item on this list. Review this list from time to time. If it's still an issue and you still cannot do anything about it, keep it parked here. Do this again and again, and after a half dozen reviews, if you still can't do anything about it, then drop it off your list completely. You might find during one of your reviews that the issue has changed and you can do something about it. In that case, "unpark it" and move it to the next list we are going to create.

4. Go to a new clean page and write at the top, *CAN DO ITEMS.* Then transfer from your first list those items you labeled *C.* For each item on this list, begin to lay out specific goal or task statements to resolve these "worries." This will be a dynamic plan, so leave lots of room beneath each listed item so you can evolve your plan and thoughts to resolve this issue. Make your task statements specific with due dates. Incorporate these items into your regular planner.

5. Execute your plan from the CAN DO list.

6. With your worries now identified and categorized, with plans made for those items you can do something about, you will be able stop obsessing or worrying about these items, knowing you have thoughtfully considered them and there's a plan in place to resolve them. You'll relax.

The main thing that happens when you take these steps above is that you are getting everything out of your head, onto paper. This step alone disentangles your mind and puts you in a better place, mentally and emotionally. When you go through the mental exercise of putting everything on paper, it makes you clarify your thoughts. You have to. You're taking a thought and turning it into a statement, bringing it into focus, all of which disentangles your mind. Your mind will go from a big jumbled morass of thoughts to a clear picture of what you're concerned about. That's healthy. Then, as you start accomplishing your steps, your mind will continue to ease.

One more thought: I'm a big believer in using the old-fashioned paper and pen. Digital journals are great and have many advantages. But when my thoughts have to go through my fingers onto a piece of paper, something wonderful happens. It takes more effort, more thought, and I think I get better results, better mental exercise, clearer pictures, and better outcomes. Do what works best for you.

I believe if you put into practice the steps I've outlined above, you'll be able to disentangle you mind, flip, and restate Corrie's quote to "use the strength of today to empty the sorrows of tomorrow."

PRINCIPLE 3

Regularly journal your thoughts, feelings, and concerns to disentangle your mind and ease the worries of life and business.

CHAPTER TWENTY-EIGHT

You Can Enjoy Your Life Now

If you're only happy when you've achieved your goal or arrived at your destination, you will have very little joy in your life.

IF YOU'RE A SMALL business owner like me, you can find yourself so immersed in the details of your business—business development, client management, employee issues (drama), cash flow, chasing receivables, managing payables—that you are constantly in "survival" mode, not "enjoying life" mode. Or maybe your personal life and the many challenges are draining your life of its energy; maybe you're having a disagreement with your spouse, your kids are not showing their best and highest selves, your weight loss program or exercise plan is failing, the car needs repair, the leaky faucet is driving you crazy. This is not the kind of life you had dreamed for yourself.

You're not having fun. You're not enjoying your life. You keep thinking, "If I can just win this new contract," or "If I can just hire that new talented employee," or "If I can just implement this new program at work," or "If my spouse will just change," or "If I can just move into a better house, or get a newer car," or blah, blah, blah . . . you get the point. We become all about the *destination* and not the *journey*. Big mistake. "Destination-only" people enjoy their lives less.

If the only time we are happy is when we have reached a destination, we will have very little joy and happiness in our lives. Destinations are few, and the happiness we feel in arriving is short lived. Whereas if we learn to enjoy the *journey*, we can be happy much more. Why? Because much more time is spent on the journey—it lasts much longer than the destination. If I am a "destination-only" kind of guy and have a goal of driving to Los Angeles, and I live in New York City, I will be miserable for five days while I drive across the country and be happy only a day when I arrive in Los Angeles. If I learned to enjoy the drive, I could be happy five more days!

You're probably thinking, "That sounds great, but how can I get out of my 'destination-only' mindset and start living and enjoying my life now as a 'journey-minded' person?" It's going to be different for everyone, but let me get your brain going with these suggestions, in no particular order.

1. Celebrate incremental wins at work or in your personal life, not just the final destination or achievement. For example, if you're responsible for delivering a major project, celebrate with your employees or team whenever you reach a milestone. This will increase morale and make the project much more enjoyable. If you're in a weight-loss program, celebrate every five or ten pounds lost. These kinds of actions will also keep you motivated.

2. Designate "off the net" time in your week. Make it a point to get off your phone, tablet, computer. Set aside this time. In my opinion, even though people today are more connected than ever, few are actually connecting. How about having a real face-to-face conversation with someone you care about? And I don't mean FaceTime them. I mean face-to-face, over a great cup of coffee in a nice cafe, sit and chat about life, sports,

shared experiences, or whatever. And again, while you're doing this, silence your phone. Be present.

3. Start a journal and write down three things every day you are thankful for. You'd be amazed at how this affects your thinking and outlook. When you do this, you don't have to think of fantastic or gargantuan things to be thankful for. It can be anything. You could be thankful for clean clothes, a comfortable home, good health, good friends, a loving family, healthy food, your teacher, the air you breathe—anything. When you start doing this, you become more present and aware of things around you. For me, I also experienced a more satisfied state of mind, less stress, and a deeper appreciation for my blessings.

4. Look back at your life. You are not where you want to be, but you're not where you used to be. Appreciate that. I can sometimes be constantly focused on what I have yet to do, to accomplish, to attain, never satisfied with what I've done or what I've overcome. This is sad. I'm not saying to obsess over your past, but pause and appreciate it. Give yourself a small pat on the back for what you've done thus far in your life. Notice I said "small" pat on the back. It's healthy to look back with an eye of appreciation for your life's path. But I wouldn't get overly impressed with yourself. That can be unhealthy, too. Be realistic and honest, but appreciate where you've come from.

5. Think about all the wonderful people in your life and appreciate them. Do something to acknowledge their role in your life. Pick up the phone and call them. Invite them to lunch, your treat. Buy them a gift—nothing big, just something thoughtful. Tell them what they have meant to you. Express your feelings for them. This kind of appreciation goes a very long way and is almost always appreciated.

6. Think about all the things that have gone right in your life. Sure, you've had setbacks. Haven't we all? But appreciate the blessings you've had. You'll be surprised at how many there are. Write them down. When you see how long your list is, you will be pleasantly surprised. You can't help but feel blessed and grateful.

7. Slow down, look around you, be present. Next time you're walking somewhere, make it a point to look around at things you normally walk by without noticing. Appreciate the storefront window, the well-kept lawn, the person going the opposite direction—say hello to them. I did this recently. As I started my walk, I decided to slow down and look around. I was surprised by what I saw. I'd made this walk many, many times yet had failed to see so much along the way. I think we do the same in life—we figuratively walk by so much without noticing its value or significance.

8. Find a good book and read it. C. S. Lewis said, "We read to know we're not alone." You're not alone. Reading about someone else's experiences can often remind us of our own condition and situation and help us see our lives from a new perspective.

9. Listen to your favorite music. I thoroughly enjoy putting on headphones, selecting a particular genre of music (and I like many genres), then closing my eyes and just listening. I can do this for hours. For me, music is so many things—therapy, encouragement, fun, mind blowing, mood altering, and just plain enjoyable. I can actually reset my mood with a favorite tune.

10. See a play, a concert, or other performance—and I'm talking about live performance. Sure, I love the movies. But watching real people, on a stage, right in front of me, perform live—

there's nothing more entertaining than that. It's more real, more alive to me. As a jazz musician, I know that a live performance is never exactly the same from performance to performance. There are little differences, nuances in each one. You're seeing a unique, one-of-a-kind performance. To me, that's special. That's really living your life.

11. Look at old photos. Let yourself smile as you do. Allow the photos to take you on a trip down memory lane, with no limitations. It can be a fun journey.

12. Write a letter to someone you love. No, not an email. Take out a real piece of paper, a real pen, and write them a letter. People appreciate this more today than ever. Express your feelings for them and what they have meant to you. This will make you both feel good. Love given and received is perhaps the greatest of gifts.

13. Create. Paint a picture, play an instrument, sculpt, draw, write. Don't tell me you aren't good enough. I've been in some of the greatest museums and galleries in the world. In my opinion, some of the stuff displayed there looks like, well, let's just say your creation can't be any worse. The point is to find a way to express your creativity. It's fun and good for you.

14. Try a new restaurant or a new dish. This is one of my favorite things to do. Yes, I do love to frequent my favorite restaurants, but discovering a new one with a different and talented chef is lots of fun, too.

There are lots more things you could do. The point is to *enjoy the journey*. Find things you enjoy doing and do them. Put them into your planner. Make the time. You can enjoy your life now, not just when you arrive at your goal or destination.

PRINCIPLE 4

Make it a point to enjoy the journey, not just the destination. You will enjoy your life more and increase your happiness.

CHAPTER TWENTY-NINE

You Can't Give What You Don't Have

"You cannot be your best if you're not at your best."

ALMOST EVERYONE WHO OWNS a small business wants to do their very best, be their very best, and give their very best. In this way they hope to somehow separate themselves from the competition or crowd. Yes, there are other business considerations in a competitive marketplace, but giving your very best is a fundamental requirement. An Olympic athlete wouldn't show up at the games exhausted, having eaten poorly for months, and dehydrated. Just the opposite is what you expect from these athletes. Fans hope to see their favorite Olympians break records, achieving greater-than-ever feats. Customers and clients are like your fans, and they hope to see the same kind of thing from you. They need to see a reason to pay you rather than your competitor. But you can't give what you don't have.

As a small business owner, I know how important it is to be at your very best, but we can often run ourselves ragged and defeat that goal. Frankly, this is one of my personal weaknesses. I have repeatedly gotten it wrong, running at a breakneck pace, neglecting my body and its needs, my mind and its needs, my family and their needs, putting myself in a horrible position—all with good intentions, of course. But as you've heard, the road to failure is paved with good intentions.

If an Olympic athlete does not allow for time to rest, time for the right kind of nourishment, time for coaching and mentoring, time to set goals, time to review his/her progress and adjust their training plan as needed, they will *not* compete at their best and highest. World-class athletes know this. You cannot be your best if you're not at your best.

One of my hobbies—serious hobbies—is jazz music performance. I consider myself an experienced jazz bassist, playing both upright and electric basses. I hesitate to use the word *hobby* because it sounds so easy come easy go. It is not that way with me. I'm serious about it. I put in hours of practice and performance each week. I'm a member of a seventeen-piece big band. I'm frequently asked to play in smaller groups. And, yes, I get paid for it—many thousands of dollars per year. I was a member of the US Navy musician program and played professionally for four years. I've performed on several albums in my lifetime, played for crowds and venues of all sizes and importance, up to tens of thousands of people, and I love it, love it, love it! I love performing.

When I'm playing, my mind cannot think about anything but playing—not work, not stress, not worries; it's a great diversion. I go to a different place mentally when performing. It's very satisfying when you've worked hard and pulled off a great performance with your good friends, and then to see the audiences respond, often overwhelmingly, is—well, it's wonderful. I'll play music as long as my body will let me. I also know exercising my creative brain and juices greatly helps me as a small business owner to see things in different ways, to consider a wider range of alternatives.

By the way, using my jazz "improvisation" skills in my business is a great advantage. I can see things, or think of things, my peers will not see or might overlook. I truly believe this. I always encourage business owners to include creative endeavors in their lives—writing, music, painting, drawing, decorating, sculpture, and so on. It will help you in many, many ways.

The point of me telling you all about my musical endeavors is to make the assertion that if I did not take the time to practice, listen to other musicians, rehearse, and keep myself musically healthy and pertinent, it would begin to show negatively in my performances and would likely result in fewer and fewer musicians inviting me to come play with them. The audiences would get smaller and smaller. My enjoyment would be less and less. I have to always make time to refill my music fuel tanks. I need new ideas, fresh approaches, and better skills.

You never reach a point where you no longer need to learn. There is always more to learn. And this doesn't just happen. There is only one basic path from novice to experienced performer—you have to work at it, all the time. There are no shortcuts, no phone apps you can download, no gimmicks that will substitute for the one who has put in the practice time. You'll hear it, very quickly, if they've not kept themselves sharp. It's the same with your life and business. If you are not investing in yourself, putting fuel back in your tank, you'll eventually have nothing left to give.

So with all that in mind, I'd like to give you some thoughts on how to stay at your best. I offer them to you for your consideration—a beginning. Use these to get your brain started down the correct path, to build your own plan that will keep your fuel tanks full, because there's nothing worse than running out of gas.

1. <u>Physical Health</u>. Properly nourish your body (the largest challenge for me), get regular exercise (and I don't necessarily mean a Marine Corps boot camp workout, but whatever you do, be consistent), get at least seven hours sleep a night. Decide how many days a week you want to exercise and put it on your calendar, then do it. Write down what you're eating every day. After a few days, study it. Have a friend study it. What's wrong with it? In my case, I love bread, cakes, and sweets. I had to

learn how to eat right. Oh, I still goof it up. But I am better, and I have lost weight. I'm not at my goal, but I am on my way. I set my bedtime and try to keep it. Again, I do goof it up, but I get back on track when I do. The main thing is *do not quit.*

2. Mental Health. Decrease the mindless activities like video games or watching too much television. Increase the mindful activities like reading, journaling, interesting conversation with a mentor or friend; learn a new skill or learn more about a current skill, or take a class. Use your creative brain, as I mentioned earlier in this chapter. Do something enjoyable, regularly, with someone you love.

3. Spiritual Health. For me this means spending time in meditation with scripture or a good book. For you it could mean listening to music, viewing art at a gallery, poetry—anything to feed your soul. Do charity work for a cause you believe in. Be a mentor to someone younger or less experienced than you. Give of yourself. Perform a random act of kindness—and do it anonymously!! How great would that be? (NOTE: Don't do the first two tips and skip this third one. I believe that this one is more important than the other two.)

Consider this. Think of your life like a checking account. You deposit money, you spend money, and hopefully you don't overdraw your account. Taking care of yourself is like depositing money in your account. Working and managing your life and business is like spending money. At the end of the day, you want to have money left in that account. You don't want to keep spending and spending without making sufficient deposits, because you will bankrupt yourself and the bank will close your account! Make sure you have money left in the bank. By the way, I've learned that the deposits tend to be small, but the spending tends to be big. It usually takes many more deposits to account for only a couple expenditures. Put another way, the money goes out faster than it comes in. Sound familiar? This is how life is for most of us.

The truth is, I'm talking to myself as much as I'm talking to you; take time for yourself, your friends, and your family.

PRINCIPLE 5

Your life is like a checking account. Taking care of yourself is like making a deposit, whereas work is like a withdrawal. Don't overdraw your account, because you can't give what you don't have. Keep a proper balance to be your best.

CHAPTER THIRTY

Keep an Attitude of Gratitude

It turns out that the benefits of having a grateful heart or attitude go way beyond just being a nice thing to have or a more socially acceptable form of behavior.

HAVE YOU EVER WORKED around someone who never seemed to say, "Thank you"? How did that make you feel? Conversely, have you ever worked around someone who frequently took the time to appreciate your efforts? And how did that make you feel? It's obvious that a grateful person is much preferred over the non-grateful. We don't always get to choose who we associate or work with, but you get my point; it's much better working with people who are grateful.

It turns out that the benefits of having a grateful heart or attitude go way beyond just being a nice thing to have or a more socially acceptable form of behavior. A quick search on Google regarding the health benefits of gratefulness reveal a large body of evidence showing the real and positive impact of gratefulness. There are also real, hardcore business benefits to showing gratitude. While it is true that "gain" isn't the only reason to be grateful, it is interesting to consider the tangible benefits of an attitude of gratitude.

Here's what I've learned through my own experiences about keeping an attitude of gratitude.

1. A grateful attitude can increase productivity through strengthened relationships and increased trust among fellow workers. When people express their thanks to each other, the bonds of friendship grow. They start to trust each other. As trust grows, people automatically drop their defenses and work collaboratively much quicker and more efficiently. They don't have to worry about everyone's motives. They feel they can work and not have to watch their back for fear of betrayal or some overzealous coworker trying to get ahead at their expense.

2. Gratefulness can increase innovation by making workers feel valued, that their ideas are important, appreciated, and welcome. No one wants to speak up and offer an idea only to get crushed by someone who publicly belittles their input. When someone says, "Thank you for that input," it encourages more input. Especially as the business owner, if you aren't showing your gratitude for your team's input or brainstorming sessions, you'll seriously stifle innovation. So beware. If you don't listen and appreciate, pretty soon you'll have no one to listen to.

3. Gratefulness has been shown in multiple studies to lower stress and increase a sense of well-being. The internet is loaded with studies showing the positive mental and emotional impacts of a grateful attitude. When people feel appreciated, they love it. Who doesn't, really? Today's millennials especially want to belong to effective teams, working toward a common goal. They want to be part of something bigger than themselves. They want to be recognized within their teams when they make an important contribution to the goal. They want connection.

Showing appreciation for their efforts helps them gain a sense of belonging. You'll also get their loyalty and devotion, which is wonderful since millennials are capable of amazing things when motivated.

4. Gratefulness will increase your mental capacity by disentangling your thoughts. When someone says thank you to me, it has a clarifying effect on my thinking. I don't feel as if I have to revisit whatever I just did because it was appreciated—job well done. I can move on. My brain can focus on other things. I can enjoy that moment, and I don't have to go back over it and obsess over what I did. It worked out well. If no one says thank you, I will wonder, "What did I do wrong?" or "That didn't work out as well as I'd hoped." It will stay with me, cluttering my mind. I may keep coming back to it, again and again, trying to settle in my mind whether I need to take any further action rather than moving on to the next thing.

5. Gratefulness will motivate people to do their very best as they feel more appreciated. I've worked for a boss who was quick to show appreciation for efforts within our organization. It made me want to work hard for him. Even if I wasn't the one getting the credit from the boss, but instead saw him give credit for the work or others, that encouraged me, too. I was happy to come to work. I was happy to put in my best effort, even work late when required, with no regrets. He was a good man. I wanted to please him.

   Conversely, I've also worked for ungrateful, self-interested bosses, and just the opposite was true; I was unmotivated, depressed, and hated to come to work. It was the same organization, same workers, same everything. The only thing that changed was one person. My good boss left for medical reasons, and the new boss arrived and turned everything on its ear. It was amazing to watch the regrettable impact of changing just the one person on an entire organization. Leaders do matter, a great deal.

6. Gratefulness will reduce conflict at work since it reduces aggressive behavior and increases empathy among workers. It's hard to be angry with a friend or someone who's shown you appreciation recently. When you have a disagreement with a coworker, and it's someone you like, it is harder to allow the disagreement to escalate into a full-blown argument because you consider them a trusted friend. You give them the benefit of the doubt. This is a good thing. Peace in the workplace is worth most any price.

What can we do to be more grateful, to show more gratitude? There are many things you can do to develop and encourage a grateful attitude. Find a time each day to write down three things you are grateful for. I do this every day, early in the morning when journaling. It doesn't have to be huge things, either. I often write down common everyday things, simple things. What's important is to start appreciating things in your life more. This will help you get into the habit. When I start my day by purposefully thinking of what I'm grateful for, it sets me up for the rest of the day with the best attitude—the attitude of gratitude.

Make it a habit to say "thank you" to someone each morning and each afternoon. It doesn't matter how small the action; being grateful will still be appreciated by the recipient. When someone opens the door or holds the elevator for you, say thank you. When someone offers to get you a cup of coffee, say thank you. When someone compliments your clothes, say thank you. When you see someone do something well, let them know: "Great job, Mary!" Consider doing it publicly, too.

Make your thank-you more tangible by sending an email, or better yet, write someone a thank-you card and put it in the mail. They will be pleasantly surprised. Tell those closest to you thank you every day. It's those closest to us that we often take for granted. On the other hand, say thank you to perfect strangers, too, for any small kindness they perform.

And if you're ready for a bigger challenge, say thank you to someone who has offended you or someone who you feel doesn't appreciate you or your work. If you can do this without any cynicism but as a pure act of kindness, you will have taken a big personal growth step. You are becoming a bigger and better person. Perhaps your kindness with be infectious and will be returned.

PRINCIPLE 6

Keep an attitude of gratitude, no matter what. The benefits are many and far-reaching.

CHAPTER THIRTY-ONE

Ten Signs You Might Be Overloaded

If everything is number one, then nothing is number one.

TELL ME IF THIS sounds familiar. You get up early, after going to bed late. You eat your breakfast, maybe. You get dressed, but you're not sure if you wore this outfit within the last few days. Your commute feels a bit like shopping at a popular store on Black Friday, fighting for position, pushing and shoving your way to work.

You arrive at work with your desk phone all lit up with voicemails. Your email inbox is depressingly full. There's a new stack of documents on your desk brandishing a yellow sticky with the words *NEED THIS TODAY!* written on them, and this stack is next to the stack you left on your desk yesterday. You look around the office, and you're sure that every single person in your open-bay-style office is glaring at you, wondering what your problem is.

You sit down, staring at your desk, depressed. You have no energy, no motivation, no desire to work. "What is wrong with me?" you ask yourself. "I used to love this job. But now all I want to do is sleep—or drink!"

You may be one of the many millions of workers who have overloaded themselves and are now suffering the consequences. You may not even be aware of it since this sinister problem can develop slowly, without warning. Even if you have the best of intentions, it can still happen. But how do you know you're overloaded? The answer is different for each person, but from my experience, here are ten signs you might be overloaded. If you are guilty of several of these, then you may need to call a time-out and regroup.

1. The first sign is the obvious one. You experience a general fatigue that you can't seem to shake. You can't seem to get to bed on time, and you can't seem to get up on time. You're always tired. You go to bed tired and wake up tired. There isn't an hour of any day where you don't feel out of gas.

2. You notice that increasingly there are a number of things you're missing: a planned meeting or phone call, something someone said earlier that you now can't remember; you lose your thought in the middle of a conversation, people's names escape you—even though you've worked with them for years. I've had people show up in my office, iPad or notebook in hand, ready to meet. I look at them with befuddled wonder. "I'm ready for our meeting," they exclaim. "What meeting?" "The meeting we discussed yesterday." And then you remember it. How embarrassing.

3. You are struggling just to maintain your primary responsibilities, rather than go above and beyond them to create, innovate, imagine, or dream. You've become the embodiment of the philosophical mantra "If minimum wasn't good enough, it wouldn't be the minimum." You've never had this attitude. You've gone the extra mile. It helped separate you from your competition. It wasn't even difficult because you loved your work. But now? You're just getting by, watching the clock for 5 p.m. so you can leave.

4. You snap at people you love and care about. This is a big indicator you might be overloaded. If you are snapping at the very people who care about you the most, something is out of balance. You need to seriously take a step back.

5. You notice the quality of your work is compromised. You find yourself taking a lot of shortcuts, delegating too much of your work, and you notice your work is often wrong or at least not quite right. It looks like a rush job, the kind of work for which you used to chastise others.

6. More and more people stop by to ask, "Are you all right?" You ask yourself, "Why does everyone keep asking me that?" You check yourself in the mirror. "Does my face look pale like I'm sick?" you ask.

7. The smallest disappointments seem enormous, emotionally. You even surprise yourself with your extreme reactions to them. Someone asks you to take a quick look at a document for your feedback, and you explode with, "What do I look like, your English professor?" And as the words are exiting your mouth, you're already thinking, "My God, what am I doing? Why am I overreacting?" You feel ashamed and guilty. Your coworker walks away stunned and hurt.

8. You have increased feelings of depression. Nothing is going right for you. Everything is difficult. Small annoyances are turning you into a real fiend. You get increasingly more sad, morose. Your self-talk is totally negative.

9. You appear to be the last one in the office or your family to know something. You're missing information, where before you did not. Everyone is excited to go to the dinner party, or family birthday party for your niece, or office reception for a recent win at work. You, however, are totally oblivious that

these events were even scheduled, but now that you know about them, you totally try to find a reason to skip them. Normally, you love these events; it is great fun to be with people you love and admire.

10. Your joy is gone. Your fire is now an ember. You have no drive. Your "get up and go" has "got up and went." You are not having fun. Work has now become work, vice your purpose or calling. You are no longer motivated to do anything, much less work.

Does any of this sound familiar? Then you may be suffering from overload. If you believe you are overloaded, then you must take steps to rebalance your life. Continuing on in an out-of-balance condition is not sustainable in the long term. You are harming yourself and most likely those you love, not to mention your business and its employees.

So what should you do? The first thing I would do is get adequate rest. Nothing else you do will be very effective if you are fatigued. When you are rested, then do a quick-and-dirty assessment of your life—get out your journal or notepad and write down all the things you are doing right now. This exercise might surprise you when you see everything written down. The next two steps are the hardest part. First, you have to put a priority on every single one of the items on your list. Number them one to however many you have on your list. And remember, everything is not a number-one priority. If everything is number one, then *nothing* is number one. Second, decide which items you can drop, and then do it. Be honest with yourself.

After this quick-and-dirty assessment, you should go back to chapter 27 and "disentangle your mind" for the longer-term fix by following the steps I've outlined.

WARNING! After you do this, do not allow things to start filling up your time again. Set your personal and professional boundaries. Anytime you allow your business and life to get out of balance, you will overload. If you start to see the signs of overload again, repeat this exercise.

PRINCIPLE 7

Entrepreneurs are prone to work overload. Regularly assess yourself. Take immediate steps to correct an imbalance, in your life and business.

CHAPTER THIRTY-TWO

Why Your Limitations Are a Gift

"I was flying by my feelings and would have flown us straight into the ground . . ."

PEOPLE LOOK AT THEIR limitations as a negative, something that constrains them or holds them back. But here's the truth: your limitations can actually be a gift. I know we don't normally consider our limitations as gifts, so let me explain. In our daily lives, we have many limits. Time only allows us twenty-four hours a day, seven days a week. Our physical bodies only allow us to do things we are healthy and fit enough to do—you can't run a marathon without being properly fit or lift heavy objects without being strong enough. I cannot design a building or paint a picture because my brain isn't wired for that. I can play a musical instrument well and often hear my friends say how they wish they could play—but they cannot due to their own musical limitations. They're great at other things, however, that I wouldn't dream of trying.

We sometimes wish we could do more and be more, and that often leads us to try to push past those limitations, to our peril. We get our bodies into trouble when we try to physically do too much, leaving us injured, sick, or worse. At work, we often try to do more than we should, beyond our capacity or purpose, and find our results are usually mediocre at best. In our personal lives, we often leave little time for rest or quality time with friends and loved ones to refresh and restore ourselves. We exceed our limits, which leads to poor outcomes for ourselves, our businesses, and our relationships. But this is looking at limits in a negative sort of way. There are positive aspects to limits. For starters, limits can save you.

When I was in training to be a private pilot, my instructor asked me to put a hooded device over my head. We were out flying on a lovely clear and cool day. This device kept me from seeing my instruments, or anything, for that matter. He then put the aircraft in a straight and level flying position. Then he said, "Now you take the controls and try to hold the aircraft straight and level without any visual references. Just use your body sensations. If you feel like you're turning or descending, try to correct it." I thought, "I can do this. If I just hold still and not move anything, I should be fine."

Well, I was horribly wrong. On my first attempt, I thought I felt the plane turning, so I made a small correction and tried to put the plane back into a straight and level position, or at least what felt like a straight and level position. When the instructor said, "Take off the hood and look where you are," I did and quickly saw I was in a normal banking turn, not straight and level. But I felt like I was straight and level. On my second attempt, I tried again to just hold still. This time it felt fine. I had no sensation of turning or descending, or anything, although I could hear what sounded like greater airflow over the aircraft, which meant I was flying faster. When he said, "Okay, take a look," I found myself in an extreme turn, pointed almost straight at the ground and gaining speed quickly! I didn't feel like I was in such a dangerous position. I thought I was fine.

I was flying by my feelings and would have flown us straight into the ground if I had not taken corrective actions. This exercise help me realize my limits as a pilot. My feelings or bodily sensations are not a good reference—they will lie to me. On a clear day, I can use my eyes to keep the aircraft level with the horizon. On a cloudy day where I cannot see the horizon, or a dark night, I need my instruments to keep me safe. I learned my limits—I cannot use my feelings to fly the airplane. Knowledge of this limitation kept me safe and alive.

Once, while traveling alone, my aircraft lost electrical power on an overcast night on a trip to Huntsville, Alabama. My engine was humming along perfectly. The onboard aircraft battery that provided emergency power to my electrical instruments lasted about half an hour, but that's it. The other non-electrical instruments were working fine, so with my flashlight, I could still monitor them and keep flying. I also had a portable GPS, with its own longer-lasting battery, and could continue to navigate just fine. I also had a handheld portable radio, which helped me continue to communicate. It wasn't strong enough to reach Huntsville directly, but a nearby aircraft could hear me and passed messages between myself and the Huntsville tower.

My instructor had actually practiced this situation with me a couple years ago, and I knew to trust my working instruments and training. I got through that emergency with no extreme actions required and landed safely in Huntsville without incident. Knowing what my limitations were, I made decisions and took actions within those limits and successfully resolved the emergency with no harm to me or the aircraft. Over the next several days, my aircraft electrical system was repaired, I finished my business in Huntsville, got back in my plane, and flew safely home.

You probably won't be faced with this type of emergency, but you'll have your own version of an emergency or life event someday. Knowing and not exceeding your limits will ensure you manage the situation properly. By the way, this principle doesn't only apply in emergencies, but in everyday life and business. By staying within your limits, you'll manage things better in all circumstances. In this way, your limits are a gift. How are they a gift?

1. Limits inform your decision-making. When you know your limits, you adjust your thinking to account for them. Your alternatives are fewer and therefore your decisions simpler. Limits provide a guardrail to keep you from running wildly off the road. For example, a budget is there to help you make best use of your resources, but also to put constraints on you so you won't overspend and put yourself in financial difficulty. It forces you to make decisions within those limits. This helps keep you safe and sound.

2. Limits can remove stress. There is comfort in knowing your limits. You don't have to worry or stress over whether to push them. You relax knowing the limit is just that, the limit. You move on. You don't have to sit and worry about what you should do. I know that my employees much prefer to know what the limits are at work—our office hours, the leave policy, who their supervisor is, the budget they are given, and other expectations in the workplace. They actually feel more secure and less stressed when they know what to expect, where the boundaries are. Not knowing what's expected of them can be very stressful, confusing, and bad for morale.

3. Limits highlight potential opportunities for learning/growth. When you reach limits, you respect them. If you wish to expand or increase your limit, learn more about the limitation in question. Seek advice, training, or more information. Improve yourself. A limit is not necessarily permanent, especially if it's a skill-related limit. It just shows you where you need to grow. When a professional sports team hits a limitation in their performance, they adjust their actions, but they also don't just accept it; they work hard to improve and overcome that limitation, to make themselves more competitive. You can do the same. Recognize, accept, and operate within your limits, but then ask yourself what can be done to overcome them.

4. Awareness of your limits can keep you safe. Just like in my pilot training story above, I knew better than to push the limit in my flying during an emergency. Staying within the limits kept me safe, making the emergency manageable. However, I only became aware of my limits through good training with a qualified flight instructor. As you consider your limits, in life or business, do so in a deliberate way such that you learn about them intelligently, under a watchful eye, safely.

So, let me encourage you to change your mindset about limits. First, tell yourself that a limitation is a gift, not a constraint. It's a good thing. Second, learn to operate within them. This sometimes takes discipline at first, but once you fully realize this is the winning approach, you will quickly and happily stay within your limits. Next, don't allow yourself to be put into a position, on purpose, where you have your limits repeatedly tested. Sometimes, this is unavoidable, but often we can avoid trouble before it happens. We entrepreneurs love to test the limits, and I agree that we should. But we should do so intelligently, with experienced people, and good planning.

Enjoy the balance and peace limitations can bring. Notice how your limitations can lower your stress. When you respect your limits, acknowledge, and embrace them, you move closer to the often elusive "balanced life." When your personal and professional life is in balance, there is no sweeter place to be. For those times where you exceed your limits, go back and think about what happened, what you can learn from it, what you do can differently going forward, and write that in your personal journal. Review it often until it sinks in. Learn that lesson. Then look for ways to expand those limits.

PRINCIPLE 8

Think of limitations not as a constraint but as a gift. Embrace and operate within them to achieve greater balance in life and business.

Part Four Recap: Hard-Won Life Lessons That Work

PRINCIPLE 1

In a conflict, the goal should be to find a way to resolve differences and move forward, for the good of everyone—*not* to win the argument.

PRINCIPLE 2

To be able to operate at your best and highest, your life-giving relationships need to be strong, happy, and healthy. Make them your highest priority.

PRINCIPLE 3

Regularly journal your thoughts, feelings, and concerns to disentangle your mind and ease the worries of life and business.

PRINCIPLE 4

Make it a point to enjoy the journey, not just the destination. You will enjoy your life more and increase your happiness.

PRINCIPLE 5

Your life is like a checking account. Taking care of yourself is like making a deposit, whereas work is like a withdrawal. Don't overdraw your account, because you can't give what you don't have. Keep a proper balance to be your best.

PRINCIPLE 6

Keep an attitude of gratitude, no matter what. The benefits are many and far-reaching.

PRINCIPLE 7

Entrepreneurs are prone to work overload. Regularly assess yourself. Take immediate steps to correct an imbalance, in your life and business.

PRINCIPLE 8

Think of limitations not as a constraint but as a gift. Embrace and operate within them to achieve greater balance in life and business.

PART FIVE:

WHEN IT ALL GOES WRONG

CHAPTER THIRTY-THREE

Stumbling Block or Stepping Stone

"They needed to forgive themselves and view that painful experience with new eyes and a fresh perspective."

THEIR BUSINESS HAD FAILED. All of the money, effort, dreams, and emotions invested in the business had come to nothing. Despite their best efforts to create the conditions for a successful venture, this couple's dry-cleaning franchise had failed miserably. Everything gone. Only painful memories and a crushing sense of defeat remained. They spent the next weeks and months wondering what had gone wrong. How could they have avoided this failure? What should they have done differently? Feelings of guilt, even shame, were constant companions in their minds.

If you've never lost a business, or anything precious to you, it can be hard to fully relate to their situation. But if you have, you know exactly what they were going through. It was painful to listen to their story, to watch their faces as they recounted this bitter experience. The wounds were deep.

Now, many years later, they were faced with another big business opportunity and had come to me for counsel. In our discussions, it became obvious to me that the franchise failure was weighing heavily on their minds, still a massive injury on their confidence. I could see that experience was holding them back, causing hesitation, making them afraid to move—in any direction—and overly cautious. It's certainly understandable, right? We should learn lessons from past failures and let it inform our future decisions. But we should not let it obstruct our path to future opportunities out of fear of failing again.

This husband-and-wife team were incredibly smart, very friendly, honest, and the kind of folks you would love to work with or even just be around. Their children were very impressive, pleasant, and loved their parents very much—that much was obvious. This told me a lot about the kind of healthy home they maintained. So my heart was very moved by their story. But I began to see that if they were to ever succeed at any venture again, they needed to give themselves permission to fail. They needed to forgive themselves and view that painful experience with new eyes and a fresh perspective. They needed to deal with it in a healthy way because, thus far, they had not.

My advice to them was this:

1. Change your thinking. They needed to change the way they viewed the whole painful franchise experience; to view it as a stepping stone, not a stumbling block; a stepping stone to success, not a failure and an end. They needed to see themselves as wiser, better informed, as a result of their experiences. They were on their way to great things, and this was a learning experience that would inform their future endeavors. One way I recommended they think about it all was this: you are either winning, or learning—you are never losing or failing. You only fail when you quit, so just don't quit. I've heard Joel Osteen, a pastor in Houston, Texas, say, "Setbacks are just a setup for your success." I agree with that. A positive attitude and perspective are so important. Whether you think you can or cannot, you are right.

2. Journal about this experience. By now you've heard me make this point again and again, but I asked them to sit down, get quiet, and journal about this experience. I asked them to write down their observations, lessons learned, things they would avoid in the future, and things they would do differently now. I asked them to write honestly how they felt when things were crashing around them and how they feel now about this new business opportunity. Someone once said, "Thoughts disentangle themselves passing over the lips and through pencil tips." Clarity comes when you take your thoughts and write them down, thoughts will organize as you turn them into words, and stress and worry is reduced.

3. Find the good. They needed to adopt an attitude of gratitude (see chapter 30) about the whole experience. Wait. What? Yes, that's what I said. Be grateful for the wisdom they now possessed as a result of this crushing defeat. You see, wisdom is a good thing and is cheap at any price, as long as you get it. It you don't, it can be very expensive.

   This experience was good for them. They are better for it. They are wiser for it. They can approach future decisions with greater confidence. Knowledge and experience will dispel fear. They definitely know more and have greater experience, so they should feel more confident, less afraid. Now, I'm not saying they shouldn't feel cautious, but there's a big difference in informed caution and worry, or considering a decision versus obsessing over it out of fear. It's the same when you compare a rookie professional athlete and a veteran. The rookie steps into a big intense moment on the field, nervous, unsure, and often fails. The veteran steps into the same situation, but using their hard-earned wisdom confidently navigates the situation to their advantage. Their wisdom improves through judgment.

   Mark Twain once said, "Good judgment is the result of

experience and experience is the result of bad judgment." How very true. Think about it. Wisdom helps us avoid bad judgment, but we get wisdom through experience, and experience through bad judgment. Chew on that for a while.

> ***"Wisdom helps us avoid bad judgment, but we get wisdom through experience, and experience through bad judgment."***

4. Dream big. Finally, I said now that they'd given themselves permission to fail and realized that this experience was part of their path to greater success and achieving their life's purpose, they should dream big! They were much smarter and wiser now. They needed to allow themselves the creative freedom to dream. All great things start with a dream. And if you're going to dream, then why limit yourself? Dream big. Get back in the game.

I am happy to report they left our meeting feeling very encouraged. They even wrote back to me later saying how much brighter everything now looked and how much easier their upcoming business decision now seemed. A year or so later, I heard from them. They had made a decision on an opportunity, stepping out in faith, and were seeing great success. In making the decision to go forward, they said they began to view their situation differently, as we had discussed, and felt more confident to make the commitment. They said they would have avoided the opportunity out of fear had they not changed their minds, forgiven themselves, and realized how much better prepared they were for this new challenge as a result of their past failure. I couldn't have been more happy for them. I know they'll do very well.

PRINCIPLE 1

Forgive yourself for past failures and see the good in them. They are a stepping stone to wisdom, better judgment, and success. Now move forward and dream again.

CHAPTER THIRTY-FOUR

Character Emerges in Crisis

"Dave's character very likely determined his fate, or at least contributed significantly to it."

"CHARACTER IS DESTINY" IS a quote attributed to the Greek philosopher Heraclitus. He implied that destiny, or fate, is not a predetermined outside force but is instead determined by your own inner character—who you are as a person. A person of great character will act differently than someone who isn't. For example, a person of character is considerate and trustworthy, someone who will do what's right even when no one is watching. Someone who lacks great character can be untrustworthy, dishonest, and will think mostly of themselves when the pressure is on—sometimes with devastating results.

I started my young professional life as a US naval officer. My first assignment was as supply officer on board a nuclear attack submarine. It was a daunting task managing the logistics support of a billion-dollar state asset, with little or no on-the-job experience. I finished near the top of my class in training and was given the opportunity to select the type of ship and job I wanted. Almost everyone who finished near the top selected submarine duty. It was considered a real boost to a young officer's career and was hard to get since there were relatively few opportunities in the submarine force. Of course, the flip side to that coin was the job was extremely challenging. If done poorly, your career might be over before it even started. I was a bit of a risk-taker, so I went for it.

Daunting as the job was, I wasn't without resources to help me get the job done. The submarine squadron my ship was assigned to existed specifically to assist us and every other ship in the squadron, and ensure their submarines were ready for war, should the commander-in-chief give the order. The squadron was staffed by very experienced submariners, with great technical expertise, who offered assistance in everything we did, from logistics to nuclear power plant management to weapons management. They were responsible for making sure we were ready for deployment, which meant they sometimes went from the role of friendly helpers to critical evaluators of our readiness, grading and documenting our ship's condition. Their inspections were also used as fodder for promotion boards, so we took those inspections seriously as our next promotion could be resting on the results. So, the squadron played a key role. My source of help and oversight was the squadron supply officer, Lieutenant Dave Smith (name changed).

Dave's job was to oversee the logistical support of all submarines in the squadron, including mine. But he went further; he spent time with me personally to make sure I was thinking about things correctly, asking the right questions of my staff, monitoring all the different levels of support for which I was responsible, designing a management approach that would work in all situations. He was very smart, highly experienced, tremendously helpful, and helped me gain great confidence in myself. In fact, I did successfully manage the logistics of the submarine, in many oceans and parts of the world, until my tour of duty ended after three and a half years of service. I owe him a great debt of thanks in large part to his watchful eye and valued friendship. He was sometimes brutally honest in noting deficiencies in my department and my management of it but was also helpful in assisting me with setting things right. He worked very long hours, usually seven days a week. I've never seen anyone more devoted. His identity was wrapped up in his job.

Dave sounds great, right? Well, he was great, for me. But there were other aspects of Dave's character I was unaware of, some bad habits he had when it came to money in the form of gambling. Over the years, I later learned, his money problems got so bad that when it was finally brought to the attention of his superiors, it was devastating to him personally and professionally. He had attained a very high level of command by then and now stood to lose his very visible public job in a very visible public fashion, which would crush his reputation and end his career, not to mention the impact it would have on his family.

It all ended tragically with Dave taking his own life. When I heard the news, I was stunned. I can only assume the horror of his situation was so great in his mind that he could not face it. We were good friends, and he had helped me so much. But when I learned the circumstances leading up to his death, I was shocked beyond belief. I had so many unanswered questions, and still do to this day. Upon reflection, I do wish Dave had realized he needed professional help and gotten it before things became bad. Nothing is worth taking your own life. It hurts even now as I write this paragraph because he was a real Navy brother to me. We enjoyed each other's company, laughed together, argued sometimes, and worked hard to support the submarine mission. I will always remember the occasional moments we had sitting aboard the submarine tender[14] in his office, just shooting the breeze, exhausted after a long week of work. They were quiet moments of camaraderie with strong cups of bad coffee—cherished memories.

Dave's character very likely determined his fate, or at least contributed significantly to it. Was his character weakness about money? That's not necessarily what I see when I look back. I think it was more about pride, the unhealthy kind. It's realizing you're not perfect—no one is—and to honestly admit when you need help. I'm sure there were other things he was dealing with, but looking back now with the advantage of time and distance, I believe Dave was a proud man and didn't like to admit mistakes—so much so that I sometimes saw

14 A submarine tender is a ship where the squadron personnel work. It contains very impressive repair and support capability.

an unpleasant side to him where his pride was concerned. He would get very upset if his reputation was ever impugned by a coworker, rather than just brushing it off and moving on. He sought to build and maintain a perfect professional image at all times. Back then I just chalked it up to his professionalism and high standards. I believe now that it was more than that.

Being a very smart man, I am sure he realized at some point before it all got out of hand that he had a problem. However, I think his pride prevented him from seeking the professional help he so desperately needed. If I'm right, this is a significant character weakness. This weakness emerged during his crisis and contributed to this tragedy. I'm not perfect, and I hesitate to stand in judgment of Dave, but I have to find a way to make sense of all this, to try to pull something useful from it so that Dave's life is not totally in vain. Can we learn something from this? I think so.

Over the years, here's what I've decided to learn from Dave's tragedy:

1. <u>No one is perfect</u>. In a competitive work environment where promotions are on the line, we try to keep our reputations clean. I understand that and believe in holding a high standard. But it's pointless to strive for perfection—which really is unattainable. While we should do our best, perfection is not a healthy goal. Rather than strive for perfection, I'd rather work to earn a reputation for excellence. This is more within reach yet doesn't suggest I have to be perfect. It keeps my standards high but also reasonable. It lets everyone know that I'm shooting high, going for the gold, but am only human and might stumble along the way. When I do, I'll get back up and keep trying to attain excellence, never quitting.

2. <u>When we do make mistakes, we should admit them early and seek assistance when needed</u>. I believe Dave knew he had a

problem—he was too smart not to realize it. But I also think he thought he could manage it on his own. He was often slow to seek advice for himself. I did observe this over the years. He obviously miscalculated and waited too late to get help. In his mind, his situation must have seemed impossible. How I wish he had sought help.

3. None of us can do life alone. We were made to do life together, in community. On board a ship, we depended on each other. The camaraderie meant everything to the officers and crew. We were made to be in family groups, of many types. We were made to be in social groups, connected by a common interest. What's the worst thing you can do to someone in prison? Put them in solitary confinement. I'm told by someone who's experienced solitary confinement that it's hell on earth, the worst thing you can do to a human being.

   When everything goes wrong, or goes to hell in a handbasket, the worst response you can have is to try to face your difficulties alone—period. I think if Dave had sought out a friend from his own community, he would have found tremendous support and been helped to a path of recovery. Instead, it appears he kept it all to himself, suffered alone, and died alone. It makes me so very sad.

On the other hand, crisis can also bring out the best in people of great character. History is replete with many stories of great men and women who overcame their own fears and shortcomings to emerge victorious in horrible situations—Apollo 13 astronauts, Medal of Honor recipients, survivors of natural disasters, and on and on.

It's kind of like a tube of toothpaste. If you want to know what kind of toothpaste is contained within the tube, put it under pressure—and out it comes. To take this illustration one step further, once the toothpaste is out of the tube, it's very hard to put it back. For the person of poor character who's shown their true colors in times of crisis, it's very hard to put things right again—not impossible, but certainly very hard.

Hopefully, when you find yourself under pressure, and you most certainly will, good things will emerge from your character to get you through. It is beyond the scope of this chapter, or even this book, to undertake a full discussion on character. In fact, it would take a whole book to treat that topic properly. But I will say that good character can be developed within us all. From my own life, I believe the things that build good character are hard work, discipline, patience, good mentors, nurturing relationships, kindness, putting others first, consistency, staying teachable, faith, good books, culture, and art. There are many other things you could add to my list, but it's a start.

I saw this quote from Abigail Van Buren, the advice columnist of Dear Abby fame. She said, "The best index to a person's character is how he treats people who can't do him any good, and how he treats people who can't fight back." I absolutely love this thought. It says so much. How you behave when no one is watching, or when you have nothing to gain, tells you something about your own character. When you consider your own character in light of Abigail Van Buren's quote, do you like what you see? How do you think you would behave? If you don't like what you see, or are afraid of what might come out of your character tube of toothpaste when pressure is applied, then it's time to do something about it. Take inventory of yourself. Look again at the short list in the previous paragraph of the things I think build character, and ask yourself if these are things you readily see in your life. If not, then it's time to get to work. If you wait to develop your character until you're in crisis, it'll be too late.

PRINCIPLE 2

Character matters and will contribute to your fate in a crisis, for better or worse. Cultivate a strong character within yourself by doing the right thing all the time.

CHAPTER THIRTY-FIVE

Keep It Straight and Level to Survive a Storm

"My flight instructor inadvertently gave me one of the most profound business and life lessons I'd ever heard."

ONE OF THE GREAT pleasures of my life was becoming a pilot with my own single-engine airplane. Yes, it was very challenging, and sometimes a bit scary, but I loved it. After several months of training, I passed my written and flight examinations and was given my private pilot license, which allowed me to fly on clear-weather days. In order to fly on days when the visibility is poor, you need an instrument rating requiring additional training and passing additional exams.

Only flying on clear days really reduces the number of days you can fly, and I wanted to use my airplane for business purposes and therefore wanted more flexibility, not less. So after getting my initial license, I immediately began working on getting the instrument rating. This would give me the skills and confidence needed to safely fly my plane using instruments only, without the aid of visual flight references like the horizon.

During my flight training, one topic that was given a lot of attention was the weather and what to do about it. As a result, I really became a student of the weather, studying weather patterns, cloud formations and their implications, and so on. The first rule I was taught was to do everything possible to avoid bad weather. But I was also taught that regardless of how hard you try, if you fly long enough, you will find yourself in difficult weather. Aviation weather forecasters, no matter how skilled they are or how powerful their computer models are, don't always get it right. Their information is helpful, but you must always consider that the weather could change without much warning. Therefore, much discussion and training centered on flying in difficult weather.

So, what do you do when you are caught in difficult weather, such as turbulent winds and rain? In turbulent weather, a small aircraft gets bounced around quite a bit, tossed back and forth, up and down, making it difficult to stay on your assigned altitude or course. For example, in only seconds, you could find yourself losing hundreds of feet in altitude from a sudden downdraft of wind. It's happened to me, and it's a bit unsettling.

The mistake the untrained pilot often makes is what my instructor called "fighting the weather." He meant that for every drastic movement of the airplane caused by the weather, the pilot tries to counter that movement in an attempt to stay on course and altitude. If the plane drops in altitude, the pilot pulls up the nose of the airplane in an attempt to climb, only to find himself now getting hit with an updraft, throwing him hundreds of feet above his assigned altitude. Now he quickly tries to lower the nose of the aircraft and decrease altitude and again gets hit with another downdraft, dropping quickly and starting the vicious cycle over again.

This can go on and on, trying to stay on altitude without any success. This puts great stress on the aircraft, wastes fuel, makes for an even more uncomfortable ride for the passengers, and distracts and tires the pilot, making him or her less effective. In extreme cases, the pilot's actions can put the small aircraft under such enormous stress fighting the weather that the plane can actually be damaged, or worse.

When my instructor explained all of this to me, I said, "Well, what am I supposed to do? This sounds very dangerous. There's got to be a solution! How do I survive a storm? You said the odds are good that one day I'll find myself in this situation if I fly long enough. What do I do?" He said calmly, "Just keep an eye on your instruments and fly straight and level. Yes, you will get tossed up and down. You may lose altitude. You may gain altitude. That's all fine. Don't fight it. Keep your plane straight and level. You may get blown off course. Fine. Straight and level. Keep this in mind, no matter what happens, and you will come out the other side of the storm. When you do come out, then get yourself back on altitude and course. If you fight the weather, you will make things worse. Just keep it straight and level no matter what the weather does."

My flight instructor had just inadvertently given me one of the most profound business and life lessons I'd ever heard. It's a lesson I've often thought about over the years. When I've been in a stormy situation in my business or life, I try not to respond each time I get tossed about by a crisis. I just hold it straight and level. I don't fight it. I try not to drastically respond to every turbulent bump as it happens. That would be exhausting, costly, and in extreme cases even dangerous. I just focus on what I know are the facts, keep the situation in perspective, don't make any drastic moves, and eventually I get through the problem—flying straight and level.

When life puts you in a stormy situation—loss of a loved one, serious trouble with one of your children, personal attacks—don't fight the storm by taking drastic actions. Like the aircraft example, just keep it straight and level, do what you know to do, maintain your routine, let your actions be determined by considered decisions that have had time to mature, and you will eventually make it through the storm. Drastic measures will only make the situation worse.

When all hell breaks loose in your business—client invoices extremely past due affecting cash flow, drama from one of your key employees, your biggest client pulls out of an enormous deal you're heavily invested in—keep it straight and level, maintain the daily rhythm at the office, take your time making decisions, step back and consider your options, don't rush into anything, don't overcorrect, don't fight the situation or do anything to make matters worse. Do what you know to do, let your decisions mature, and after considering all reasonable alternatives, move ahead deliberately, as calmly as possible. Yes, you may have to make some tough choices, but only make them when you are in a good place mentally and emotionally. Remember the HALT acronym? Don't make big decisions when you are hungry, angry, lonely, or tired.

Keep it straight and level and you will come out of the storm. Then, when you do, if you're off course and altitude, that's the time to make corrections. Once when I was flying from Ohio to Virginia, the weather deteriorated on me rapidly, so much so that I began to search for an airport to land and wait it out. But before I could make that happen, I was in the clouds, getting tossed drastically up and down. I remembered my training and just held the plane level. I was changing altitude by hundreds of feet, up and down, in only seconds. I let the winds do whatever they were going to do. I did not fight it. If I got pushed up a few hundred feet, I let it happen but kept the plane level. If I got pushed down a few hundred feet, I let it happen and just kept the plane level.

I did try to gently steer toward what looked like better weather conditions. But I kept going the same general eastward direction. Eventually, within about five long minutes, I came out the other side of the turbulent air into smooth air. Interestingly, my altitude was very close to my original altitude, even though I had just been on quite a roller-coaster ride. By keeping it straight and level, the ups and downs all equaled out. Who knows where I would have been had I tried to correct for each and every up- or downdraft of air?

When you are in your storm, don't respond to each and every drastic wind. Just hold it straight and level. You may find, like I did, when you emerge from it all, you're right where you wanted to be anyway. Don't forget that just like drastic moves can overstress the aircraft, drastic moves can overstress your life and business, too.

Stay calm and keep it straight and level.

PRINCIPLE 3

When the storms of life and business toss you to and fro, don't fight the storm with drastic actions. Keep it straight and level, and you will come through it.

CHAPTER THIRTY-SIX

One of the Greatest Threats to Your Business

"The moment you stop learning, you stop leading."

—Rick Warren

IF YOU'RE IN BUSINESS, you've no doubt learned that there are a multitude of threats you must deal with, of every variety and strength. For example, there are the obvious threats such as insufficient financial resources, not finding and retaining the right talent, competition, market fluctuations, evolving tax law, and regulatory compliance issues. However, there are also the less obvious and softer threats that can be even more significant, such as poor company culture and the shifting winds of consumer fads and trends.

But to me, there is perhaps no greater threat to your business than *you*. What? Yes, *you*, especially if you're the business owner and founder, the vision-caster, the creator or responsible leader of the enterprise. If you are indeed the leader, you cannot take your business beyond where you are intellectually, emotionally, creatively, even morally. You are the constraint. So my question to you is this: what are you doing to become a better version of you, to increase your knowledge, your understanding, your people skills, and your vision? If the answer is nothing, then your business will go no further than you.

"You cannot take your business beyond where you are."

But you might say, "Wayland, I hire the best and brightest people, and they will take us to the next level." Maybe. However, often I've seen bright, motivated people stymied by a leader who has quit growing and learning. Like Rick Warren once said, "The moment you stop learning, you stop leading." Are you limiting the talented people around you because of your lack of knowledge, your unwillingness to learn or change, and your closed mind?

Your unwillingness to learn and grow can lead to multiple problems and weaknesses, such as the following:

1. A lack of respect and consideration for other opinions or perspectives.
2. An inability to consider that you might be wrong about something.
3. An inability to manage your ego.
4. Failure to examine and honestly acknowledge your motivations for certain actions or decisions you make.
5. Failure to be honest with yourself.
6. Failure to affirm and maintain your own integrity.
7. Taking it personally when confronted by an employee or colleague.
8. Failure to trust your people.
9. Inconsistency and incoherence in your leadership.

Napoleon, during a streak of victorious battles, lived by a set of maxims he wrote himself. They proved to be amazingly accurate and powerful when followed. Yet when things began to go against him, his advisors tried to recommend courses of action that would have turned the tide back in his favor, simply repeating Napoleon's own rules and maxims to him. But his failure to listen, to consider he might be wrong, closed his mind to their advice—and it was his own advice. How astonishing. Napoleon continued to break his own proven rules in battle, and he lost everything. Not staying teachable, not keeping an open mind, led to his demise.

Don't become the weakest link in your business's chain. Below are some strategies to keep yourself moving forward, growing, and learning rather than becoming the greatest threat to your business:

1. Make time daily for yourself. I know I've mentioned journaling many times in this book, but guess what, I'm going to mention it again. I believe it's that important. Journal daily about your goals, your feelings, how you're feeling about your feelings, decisions to consider, things you're grateful for, ideas you thought of, anything that comes to mind. Putting things down on paper will help to disentangle your mind and free it up to think about the critical things.

2. Make time to read good books. Last year I read over forty books. It was not difficult. In fact, it was very satisfying. It also paid big dividends in expanding my mind. I took some of the ideas that I read and adapted them into programs and activities in which we now benefit. Read a mix of business and professional books, as well as quality novels. I get so many ideas when I read. My mind is always opened to things it wouldn't otherwise consider when I read. One more tip: when you read, keep your journal or a notebook handy. Thoughts will come as you read and you'll need to jot them down immediately or you'll likely forget them.

3. Listen/watch reputable podcasts and videos. Hear what thought leaders are thinking. Listen to a variety of them, both professional and personally interesting topics. For example, I

often listen to business podcasts, but I also love podcasts on leadership, hiking, jazz music, and more. Podcasts are great when you commute. Make use of that time. Again, keep your journal handy and scribble down those thoughts as they appear.

4. Attend useful conferences and classes. Increase your knowledge in your area of expertise, and network with others in your field. Conferences are great places to share ideas, and learn what folks are thinking and where new trends are developing. Take a class in something you've always wanted to do. Not only have I attended conferences related to my work, but I also took classes and learned to sail, play golf, write a novel (which I hope to do very soon), and cook like a gourmet. These kinds of activities make you a more interesting person and open up new dimensions to your thinking, which will benefit you in everything you do. You become more and more a benefit to your company and your family, rather than a threat or a dead weight, when you expand your mind and your world.

5. Cultivate personal relationships with people you respect. They will challenge you and hold you accountable to your own goals. If they are willing, make them a mentor. Meet with them regularly to discuss your goals and dreams. We all need someone with whom we can be completely honest, discuss crazy ideas before we make them "official" ideas, and someone who'll speak the truth to us in a caring way.

You are the key to great things for your organization or business. But you must remain teachable—open minded and willing to listen and learn. You must cultivate a personal culture of learning and growth. Others will see it and not only respect you for it but also try to emulate it. This will empower people all around you. When the conductor of an orchestra raises his baton and signals the start of a piece of music, he or she sets the tempo, not the musicians. If the music is going to work, to be enjoyed, everyone must perform at the conductor's tempo. You are like that conductor. Everyone is watching you for the tempo. Are you ready and up to the task? Do you know the music? Have you practiced it? If you're not ready, it will hold back the entire orchestra. They can only move with you, not ahead of or behind you.

Imagine a bicyclist pedaling up the hill. If he keeps pedaling, he will eventually get to the top. It will be hard, but it's only a matter of time and he'll succeed. If he stops pedaling, his momentum might carry him a few feet further, but he will start rolling backward. Business and life are the same. Like the cyclist, you are either pedaling up the hill and progressing or doing nothing and going backward—*there is no standing still.* You are either growing or going backward.

Keep pedaling. Keep learning. Keep growing. Stay teachable. Don't hold back your team.

PRINCIPLE 4

Stay teachable, always learning and growing with an open mind. You cannot take your business beyond where you are.

CHAPTER THIRTY-SEVEN

Greatness From a Great Mess

MY CAREER WAS OFFICIALLY in a shambles. My boss was standing right in front of me, wearing a very grim face. He had just told me that he no longer wanted me in his office, that I was a big disappointment to him, and that he would transfer me to any other location I chose as long as it wasn't his office.

I was devastated. I had tried very hard to please my boss, but I just wasn't able to. I could give you many stories and reasons for what had happened and why I was in this predicament, but that's not the focus of this chapter. I'd rather discuss what I did going forward, making something good out of this horrible situation.

I will say, however, concerning the events leading up to my firing, that my career had been on the success fast track for fifteen years, which was why I was working in this man's office in the first place. He was one of the most senior officers in our enterprise, a man of great influence and intellect, very successful in his own right. I earned my position with him, picked from a host of candidates to work for him. But it ended up going very wrong, as I've described.

I'd like to say that I had an immediate plan going forward, that it was detailed, well thought out, vetted, but that would not be true. I had no clue what I was going to do. My mind was somewhat blank from the shock. How could I have gone from "one of the most promising" employees, according to my last performance evaluation, to "I no longer want you in my office"? I was experiencing whiplash with this surprising turn of events.

Here's basically what I did:

1. Personal Support System. I ran to my wife and family. I shared my disaster. I needed time to process all of this, and my wife and family helped me tremendously, expressing their love and support. My wife is my biggest fan, an experienced personal coach, my confidant, my strength. She spoke so much encouragement to me that after some time with her, I felt like I could now face the coming days, whatever the difficulty. My kids reminded me that I am not my circumstances. My identity is not in my work or profession, but in my character—who I am, not what I am. I was the same person yesterday as today. They loved me, said they believed in me, that this was only temporary, and I would bounce back stronger than ever. I cannot tell you how important my family is to me. This event only proved it, once again.

2. Renewed Faith. I took time to process the situation, think about all the success I had achieved in my career thus far, and put things in perspective. I was not a loser. I was capable of great things. Because my family "put me right" again in my attitude, I began to think rationally about myself and my future. As a man of faith, I also went to scripture and found incredible strength there. I found stories of people who had overcome extreme circumstances, and these circumstances became a part of their new purpose and success. The setback wasn't a problem but rather part of the new vision and purpose. My faith in myself was renewed.

3. Evaluate the Situation. I now began to evaluate the situation and consider the various alternatives. My boss had given me an

offer to move to another office—a potentially important step to a career recovery. I also had good friends within the enterprise who were ready to assist me. I knew of several projects that I'd previously thought would be enjoyable to pursue. I listed all the opportunities I believed were available to me. I let my mind go, to dream of the new possibilities.

I'd heard many times before of successful people who'd tell you that the best day of their lives involved the tragic events that led them to their current purpose and profession. Had they not been fired or moved to a different office, they would have never had the current opportunity they are now successfully living. Their failure or calamity was the catalyst of their current success. I decided that the same could be true for me. I had several good, viable opportunities from which to choose.

4. Decide and Move Forward. After talking with my family, my friends at work, and a mentor, I made a decision and moved forward. I told my boss I'd like to move into a consulting position within the organization. He laughed at me and said, "Well, you just confirmed how stupid you are by choosing that position. You'll go nowhere there. I gave you an opportunity to go anywhere and you chose poorly." As surprising as that comment was, what surprised me even more was that I was unshaken by his comments. I was confident in myself and my choice.

As you may have gathered by now, my boss was a difficult man—an eccentric. High achievers are often eccentric, but also highly intelligent with great vision. I had a great deal of respect for his abilities and innovative approaches to problem-solving. I had learned a great deal from him, so I have never regretted working for him. I could have taken a dim view of him, been personally offended by him, but I decided to view the glass as half full, not half empty—keep the good, and toss the bad. Just because he was a horrible person doesn't mean his ideas were horrible.

So, what happened? The consulting position I chose turned out to be one of the best decisions I've ever made. It lead to the formation of my own successful company over twenty years ago. Without my boss firing me, I would not be enjoying the success I have today. To his credit, my boss had a very innovative idea on how to assess an enterprise's supply chain and logistics capability. He had tried to get this idea off the ground, and I had the advantage of working on this project with him, seeing it all firsthand. Even though he abandoned the idea after a few attempts to get traction with it, I thought it was marvelous and only needed a little tweaking.

After a year in the new consulting position, I left the enterprise and started my company with the sole purpose of offering his approach to logistic assessments, with my new tweaks. I got my first contract very quickly, and the rest is history. Tens of millions of dollars later, we've sold our services to the US, UK, Canada, and Australia. We've done work in other countries as well, but those were the biggest customers. We moved from this into customized logistics decision support software and have continued to grow at a steady, sustainable pace. It was one of the best times of my life, working with the best professionals I've ever known—my team of employees. They are wonderful, hardworking, innovative people. I'm so glad my boss fired me.

By the way, after I had hit my stride and was a successful company, I had the opportunity to inform my old boss of what I'd done. I wasn't sure what he'd say. Part of me thought he'd demand a royalty payment or something. I was a little worried. Again, to his credit, he said that I deserved the success. He said he wasn't able to monetize the idea, but I did. My improvements to the idea were the reason it was succeeding. I was able to envision something he did not. He wished me every success, and yes, he did admit perhaps he had been a little hasty dismissing me. I was so glad I had closed the loop with him, because soon after that conversation, he passed away from ill health. I am grateful we spoke and parted on good terms.

If you are currently facing a disaster in your life or career, think about the story above. You can recover like I did. You might take a different path than me, but consider the recovery I made by running to my support system, renewing my faith, stepping back and evaluating the situation, and making a decision to move forward. Your story will be different, but it can all turn out well for you—and even better than it did for me. You can see greatness from a great mess.

PRINCIPLE 5

Setbacks are not permanent and do not define you. Change your mind. Make your setback part of your next success.

CHAPTER THIRTY-EIGHT

Learning From Your Bad Boss

"I've learned just as many valuable lessons from my bad bosses as from my good bosses—maybe even more!"

ONE OF THE GREAT things about serving in the US Navy was all the quality leaders you get to know and learn from. I believe some of the best and brightest leaders America has to offer are in the military services. But I can also say from personal experience that there are also leaders who do the service no credit whatsoever—those who embody the worst kind of example or ideal.

Thankfully, I only experienced a couple of those poor leaders in my twenty-year career. However, I can say with great conviction that I learned as much or more from the poor leaders as from the great ones. In fact, I would even be tempted to say that I learned more *valuable* lessons from the poor leaders.

While serving aboard a nuclear attack submarine, my first commanding officer embodied all the good qualities you find leadership authors writing about: courage, vision, passion, fairness, concern for your fellow man, the virtue of hard work, leading from the front rather than behind, a man that inspired his officers and senior enlisted men to be the best at what they did and to develop their subordinates for future greatness. Our boat received many awards from our upper echelons, those responsible for ensuring our readiness for combat. We were awesome! Our morale was high. The team spirit on board was great, too. The culture and attitude of the crew was like a brotherhood, each man looking out for the next man. The work was hard, the hours long, but the satisfaction of doing something so vital to national security with talented people you respect was amazing.

I felt part of something quite special. Besides living and working on a truly amazing engineering and scientific masterpiece, a submarine was exciting. A submarine is an amazing thing when you think about what it took to envision it, design it, build it, and then sail in it. These were real innovators, visionaries, and explorers. I felt like we were "underwater astronauts." With the exception of outer space, perhaps no environment remains as unexplored or as mystical as the sea. Even though we've learned a great deal about the sea and operating beneath it, there is still so much more we don't know. I felt like I was on the leading edge of technology, a crew member of an amazing technological feat, and I was proud to be there. Whenever my wife and I were out and about, with friends or at church, people would usually act very interested when I said I worked aboard a submarine. It was rewarding and gratifying to be doing something so unique that few would ever have the chance to do.

One horrible day, we got the word that our captain was very ill and would have to be relieved of his command to receive medical attention. As you can imagine, if anyone in the crew has a medical condition of any kind that could possibly become a problem while we're at sea, they have to be removed since we have no doctor on board or medical facilities. We did have a corpsman, like a nurse, who was very talented and could do quite a bit in an emergency but wasn't a physician. So, if we ever had a serious medical emergency, it could be a real problem. Our captain's condition was one that wasn't visibly obvious but could flare up without warning and become serious. He had to be relieved of command. It was too risky for him.

The Navy sent us a new captain. In his very first meeting with the officers of our wardroom, he said, "Do you all know why you're here?" After a brief silence, he continued, "You're all here to make sure I get promoted. Whatever you do, do your jobs well and put me and this ship in the best light possible with our squadron commander. If you do not, you will pay the price." We were dumbstruck. What had the sea gods just done to us? Even though we knew things were about to change for the worse, we had no idea how bad it was going to get.

Like I mentioned about our previous captain, our new captain was also many of the things you find leadership authors writing about, but in the negative sense: bureaucratic to a fault, an accomplished micromanager, no vision, perceived as unfair by the crew in his management style, with no concern for anyone but himself and his own career. This quickly resulted in the officers going from a team attitude to an attitude of every-man-for-himself. The captain often pitted one officer against the other, tearing down any team-oriented culture we had. He would worry about the smallest, most unimportant details of life aboard, then gloss over the major issues of operating a nuclear submarine—majoring on the minors, and minoring on the majors, as we say.

He treated his lovely wife terribly, right in front of us. Once while at a "mandatory fun" dinner at his house with our wives, we were invited into the backyard for a friendly game of volleyball—or so we thought. The teams were divided up, and we began playing. After a few moments, the captain's wife, who had no athletic ability at all but was a joy to be around, missed a couple of very easy volleys. No big deal. We are all laughing and having fun. No one was keeping score, or so we thought. The captain publicly humiliated his wife in front of us for missing those volleys. It was so awkward. She had tears in her eyes. We were dumbstruck, again.

In only a few months, we went from award-winning and awesome to below average and just meeting the minimums in readiness. Remember, this was the same ship, same crew. Only one man changed—the captain.

I was taught an invaluable lesson on the impact and value the right leader can have on an organization. It was incredible! Truly amazing to actually watch! Hard to describe unless you were there, but I hope you can use your imagination and appreciate what I'm describing. As I always try to do when I face challenges, here are a couple lessons I learned during my time with our new captain:

1. <u>Having the right person in charge is critical</u>. You can have the best team ever assembled, but if the leader is a loser, there's little chance for the team to be its best and highest. Now whenever I make a decision to put a leader in place over a project or team, I reflect on what happened on my submarine. I want to make sure I pick the right person. I know how important it is. Also, reflect on what I said in chapter 36, that you, the leader, are one of the greatest threats to your business. You must stay teachable and open minded, striving to keep learning and adapting to your market.

2. <u>Also, if you have a superb leader but the team is only average, the leader can make the whole team superb</u>. That's what good leaders can do. Our first captain took over an average crew and turned it into an award-winning sub. That all changed when he left. He was the critical factor. He set the tempo, the culture, and the vision. He caused the crew to believe they could achieve great things, and they did.

When you find yourself working for a poor leader, don't just dismiss them—take notes. My second captain showed me how *not* to do things all the time, especially when it came to people. That has informed my approach to leading people for many, many years since. Knowing what poor leadership habits look like has been critical to my success.

I met the new captain many years later in the halls of the Pentagon. He had somehow gotten promoted once more, but I believe his career was almost over by that time. When we chatted in the hallway, he quickly recalled some of the days we had together. We shared information about other crew members we knew. We compared notes on the Defense Department's current strategic direction and made other small talk. He was carefree, content with his submarine command. After saying goodbye, I was struck by the whole tone of his conversation, as if nothing were wrong, all our memories were good ones, assuming my experience was the same as his. He obviously felt his time on board was great and everyone recalled those days like he did.

Some people just don't get it and may never get it. He seemed oblivious to how he came across. I didn't take those moments to unload on him and tell him what I really thought. My parents always taught me that if you have the choice to be kind or right, be kind. So I was kind and kept the conversation civil, even though my heart was beating out of my chest, angry at this man who caused such horrible memories.

PRINCIPLE 6

You can learn as much or more from poor leaders as good ones. Let them show you how *not* to do things. It can be very valuable and inform your future as a leader.

Part Five Recap: When It All Goes Wrong

PRINCIPLE 1

Forgive yourself for past failures and see the good in them. They are a stepping stone to wisdom, better judgment, and success. Now move forward and dream again.

PRINCIPLE 2

Character matters and will contribute to your fate in a crisis, for better or worse. Cultivate a strong character within yourself by doing the right thing all the time.

PRINCIPLE 3

When the storms of life and business toss you to and fro, don't fight the storm with drastic actions. Keep it straight and level, and you will come through it.

PRINCIPLE 4

Stay teachable, always learning and growing with an open mind. You cannot take your business beyond where you are.

PRINCIPLE 5

Setbacks are not permanent and do not define you. Change your mind. Make your setback part of your next success.

PRINCIPLE 6

You can learn as much or more from poor leaders as good ones. Let them show you how *not* to do things. It can be very valuable and inform your future as a leader.

PART SIX:

ADDITIONAL WISDOM AND INSIGHTS

CHAPTER THIRTY-NINE

The Beginning of Wisdom

The more you know, the more you realize how little you know.

I HEARD JOYCE MEYER, a nationally known Christian author and public speaker, say recently that she was increasingly convinced that "nobody knows anything until they're forty years old." Catching my attention, she went on to add, "That's because when you reach forty, you begin to realize something—that you really don't know anything! And this is the first sign of real intelligence."

I got a good laugh out of that statement, especially when you realize there's often important truth buried in a lighthearted joke like that, and this was no exception. For my own part, I came to a similar observation about myself around that age. It seemed the more I knew, and the more I learned, and the more experienced I became, the more I realized I didn't know much at all! And according to Joyce, that would be when I began to show real intelligence and real wisdom.

King Solomon wrote a proverb in scripture that says, "The fear of the Lord is the beginning of wisdom." To me, this statement simply acknowledges that we humans really don't know very much, that there is always someone else who knows more, and if we are wise, we will respect that fact and conduct ourselves accordingly. We should keep our minds open, acknowledge other opinions, look for alternatives to our own theories, ask hard questions, never stop learning, and seek knowledge any and every way we can.

In addition, I think Solomon was also implying another very important attribute that truly mature, emotionally healthy, and wise people will have: that of humility. There is so much out there to know—so much, in fact, that all knowledge is unknowable. Your head can't hold all possible knowledge—far from it. Once you realize this, you are truly "getting it." When you humbly approach life with this belief, your path is much different from the one who believes they know it all. You begin to realize that you need others, their perspectives, their knowledge, their advice. Alone you are limited, constrained only by what you know. When you work with others, you are less constrained and better positioned to succeed. Your collective knowledge is greater, more powerful, giving you greater potential.

I am reminded of an important principle I discussed earlier in this book: that the outcomes in our lives are driven by the decisions we make, and the decisions we make are driven by the things we believe. If our belief system is flawed, our decisions will be poor, and the outcomes will be, well, not what we would hope. So, if you believe you know it all, then your decisions will be based on what you alone know. But if you believe "you don't know anything," your decisions will be informed by your constant search for knowledge and information, new ideas, and other learned opinions and perspectives, thereby raising the chances for your best and highest outcomes.

How does one get wisdom? Is wisdom "gettable?" Or is it something you just have or you don't? I'm happy to say that wisdom is in fact "gettable" if you have the right attitude. Some wisdom can be learned from good books or stories about great leaders, but in my life, most of the wisdom I've learned, if it can be said I've learned any wisdom, has come from my own personal experiences. I learned it the hard way, in the school of hard knocks. I think most people learn wisdom this way. The great thing about wisdom is it can keep you from bad decisions. But that's also where wisdom is learned—from bad decisions.

I'd just won an incredible contract. Ah! Winning—it never gets old. I love it! Don't you? But what you don't know is that the road to this contract win wasn't all that fun. I had several scars and bruises to show for it. There were several hideous losses on the way to this win. It wasn't pretty. In fact, it was a bit ugly. I made several mistakes: a partnership gone terribly wrong, an incredibly poor job of assessing the competition on a contract bid, a complete miss on interpreting the client's requirements, an unbelievably horrible job of choosing and assigning people to a contract opportunity.

This was a costly road, too. All of these lessons were expensive. Or were they? My father used to say, "Wisdom is cheap, at any price—*if you get it*. If you don't, then it can be very expensive." Each of those bad experiences I just listed above was a learning experience. They were steps on the road toward my winning destination. The key was to make sure I learned the lesson and did not repeat it. I've heard it said that "you're either winning, or learning." I love that. When you lose, you don't necessarily lose . . . you can learn and thereby turn it into a win by avoiding the mistake next time. The experience will inform your next moves. Just make sure you learn the lesson. If you don't, it can be doubly painful.

I can think of many opportunities since that contract where I've made better decisions and avoided past mistakes. I'm wiser and better informed. So wisdom is cheap at any price, if you get it. Just make sure you learn your lessons and get the wisdom from your bad decisions. To assist you, here are the steps I followed after my mistakes on the contract above to get the wisdom from it.

1. <u>I stepped back for a brief time</u>. How long you step back will be situationally dependent, but mentally and physically step back. Get out of the office. Go for a walk. Have lunch with your spouse or significant other—someone who gets you and

can speak into your life and encourage you. The goal here is to get back to a place of emotional stability after your setback or mistake. You can't think straight when the environment is noisy, or you are emotionally upset, or you don't feel well. Make sure you're in a relatively quiet place, in a relatively healthy state of mind. I like to grab a really good cup of coffee and sit outside on my deck at home.

2. I recorded what just happened. In your quiet place, write in your journal what just happened. Record all the details: the client, the opportunity missed, the circumstances, everything. Journaling again, Wayland? Yep. What? You don't journal? You should! No, you must! Writing will clarify what happened, sort your thoughts, and begin the process of making sense of it all.

3. I discussed it with my mentor. If you don't have one, get one. You need fresh eyes, fresh brainpower, new blood looking at what just happened. Get their perspective on these events, and their recommendations. Your mentor must be someone who knows their stuff, cares deeply about you, and will be brutally honest. They should have your permission to hold you accountable for your decisions. Your meetings should be planned and regular, not ad hoc and whatever, whenever. It should be a deliberate effort.

4. I identified the lesson and learned it. If you could do it over, what would you have done differently? What should you do going forward? Where did you make your mistake? Are there different people you should have involved? How could you have avoided it? Write each lesson learned. Now listen closely. If you don't include the answer with each question, the new approach for each mistake, you've only identified your lessons, not learned them. Learning your lesson means you've decided what you will do in the future the next time this happens. Make

sure you write down (1) the problem or mistake and (2) the recommendation or new approach for next time.

5. I brought my team together to discuss the mistakes. All of those involved need to talk about this with you. They need your thinking, and you need theirs. Their feedback will be important to ensure you've pulled out all the lessons that can be learned, but to also get their buy-in going forward. You and your team need to be united. Unity is powerful. Discuss and update your lessons learned with them and ensure everyone gets a paper copy of what was agreed.

6. I used these lessons to inform our future strategy and next moves. When we next sat down to look at our strategy as a firm, or our strategy for a particular contract proposal, or anything else, we reviewed our lessons learned and used them to inform our future strategies. It impacted our thinking and decision-making, which in turn positively affected our outcomes.

7. I then executed our new strategies. We moved forward better positioned to succeed, and succeed we did. We were now wiser, smarter, and more prepared.

By the way, we did make more mistakes, but we included them in our next round of discussions as new lessons learned. You never stop learning and improving, because you don't know it all—this is the beginning of wisdom.

PRINCIPLE 1

The more you know, the more you realize you how little you know. This is the beginning of wisdom. Let this inform your future.

CHAPTER FORTY

Entrepreneurial Lessons From the Military

"First lesson from the military is teamwork. It's not about you. It's about others first."

WHAT DID THE MILITARY teach this entrepreneur? What could the military possibly teach any entrepreneur? Isn't the military all about "obey, obey, obey" your superiors and no free thinking allowed? Isn't entrepreneurship all about innovation, challenging established thinking and the status quo? It doesn't sound like there would be a rich learning environment for the entrepreneur in the military. And if that's what you think, then let me try to enlighten you.

For some context, you should know that I am a retired US naval officer. I served during the Cold War aboard USS *Baltimore* (SSN-704), an attack submarine. The "SSN-704" thing is the hull number of the ship—all commissioned US Navy vessels have them, and it identifies the ship and its basic purpose or mission. During Operations Desert Shield and Desert Storm, I served aboard USS *Mars* (AFS-1), a surface ship. I also did a four-year tour of duty in the Pentagon. After retirement I started and grew a successful management consulting firm, which lasted over twenty years. So I am both a veteran and an entrepreneur.

I can state, without reservation, that the military taught me so many things that have been incredibly beneficial as an entrepreneur—critical things. Let me share some of them with you.

Lessons for Entrepreneurs From My Military Service

1. It's not about you. Aboard ship, whatever we did, it was always about the crew. Sure, we took very good care of the ship. It was an awesome technological platform, but without a trained and healthy crew, the ship meant nothing—it was useless. Your plans and actions centered on them—their safety, their training, their welfare. In this way, a ship could be truly great. In fact, if others ever called your ship great, they weren't talking about the steel, the computers, the weapons, the design, and so forth; they were talking about the crew.

   In business, as the entrepreneur or business owner, your attitude must reflect this lesson concerning your team or employees. Everything should be about them—your work, how you spend your time and money, should be about others: your employees, your clients, your loved ones. Don't make it all about you. Aboard ship, it wasn't all about the captain. Good captains knew this, and instead of creating a culture where everyone served them, good captains became the servants of their crews. This always had a tremendous positive impact on morale. Who wouldn't want to work for a captain that showed more concern for you and the crew than he did for him or herself? You'd follow that captain into hell and back. Someone who can inspire that kind of devotion and loyalty is indeed a great leader. There was the other kind of leader, too, who did make it all about them, and I witnessed the exact negative opposite in crew performance and morale. So don't make your business all about you.

2. The harder you work, the luckier you get. This is almost self-explanatory. Running a ship and running a business are exactly the same when it comes to the kind of luck we're talking about here. You always have better "luck" or fortune the harder you work, the more time you spend preparing or planning, the more effort you put into training. If someone ever said, "Aw, he did so well because he was just lucky," I guarantee you that if you looked closely, you'd find someone who spent long hours preparing, learning, creating the conditions for something awesome to happen.

   We had another saying aboard ship: "Expect what you inspect." This meant that those who were out and about, constantly checking on their people and the conditions of the part of the ship they were responsible for maintaining, talking with their people—those were the ones rarely surprised by a problem within their domain. Also, the crew knew that you'd be out and about looking and checking their work, so they'd try just a little harder to make sure things were done right, looked tidy, and were ready for action. Again, this would also be the same for your business. To take a "set it and forget it" approach is to invite trouble into your business. Besides, you should be out and about, touching your people, talking and listening to them. While you're doing that, keep your eyes open to ensure all is well.

3. Accept nothing less than the best from yourself and those around you. One of my favorite leadership maxims is "do as I do" not "do as I say." Don't expect anything more from your employees than you are willing to do yourself. Your people need to know this, without question. If you find yourself asking them to put forth an extreme effort for a task at hand, they should know that you aren't asking them anything that you yourself wouldn't be willing to do. There's nothing wrong

with high standards. Just make sure those standards apply to yourself first, then to your team. When you are the kind of leader who's willing to get your hands dirty, then you can rightfully ask your people to put in an extraordinary effort for the job at hand. If you hold yourself to high standards, then you can rightly ask the same standards of your team. But if you're one of those "do as I say, not as I do" type of leaders, resentment can build and morale suffer, not to mention the results of your work. Expect the same from your team that you expect from yourself.

4. Know your team and associates, their strengths and weaknesses. This lesson is essential if you are to get the best and highest out of your team. A coach for any team sport knows that to get the best results, you need to know strengths and weaknesses. Only when you know this can you properly utilize players. For example, you might want to adjust the way you pair each player with an opponent's player, to take advantage of a strength. In business, knowing a strength, you'd put the best "athlete" in the best position to succeed, based on the requirements and conditions of the task.

   Carefully aligning each person to the right task to maximize their performance sets up your best chances for success, and the employee will enjoy it more, too. Emphasize and utilize their strengths, and work to improve their weaknesses. Don't just accept a person's weakness. Encourage them to acknowledge the weakness, then provide a means to improve it. Again using the coach analogy, when a weakness is discovered, the coach will work on that weakness to improve it, not just accept it and say, "Oh well, can't be helped." Most people will welcome the chance to improve themselves, if given the chance. Give it to them. You'll both be glad.

5. Communicate, communicate, communicate. Your team needs to know what you're thinking and where the organization is headed. You have to tell them and keep them updated. You limit your team, otherwise. Aboard ship there were multiple ways things were communicated, at multiple levels, but it all began at the top. The captain would daily put out his intentions for the day. He would discuss longer-term plans weekly. But once the officers knew the captain's intentions, they would then apply them to their areas of responsibility and make sure their plans reflected his intentions.

   For example, before you took control of driving the ship, you would review the captain's plans for the ship that day. In this manner, you could facilitate and prepare the ship to perform properly and carry out the captain's orders. This multilayer approach to communication ensured every crew member, from the most senior officer to the most junior enlisted member, knew what the captain's intent was. Consequently, whatever was done that day or throughout the week would be in alignment. It didn't always work perfectly because the ship was manned by human beings prone to mistakes, or the ship would get orders from higher command, changing our assigned mission and negating the captain's plans. In your business, it's also imperative that everyone, top to bottom, understands your intentions. You may not need the level and frequency of communications we had aboard ship, but you do need some level of communication. When everyone understands what's going on and what's expected, it's a beautiful thing. By the way, it's also a big morale booster.

6. Develop your team, then get out of their way. One of the greatest lessons I learned is to build the best team you can, tell them what needs to happen, then get out of their way. You'll be amazed at what they can do—what they are eager to

do. If you've done your job well, do them and yourself a favor: get out of their way! Oh sure, check in from time to time, but leave them to it. You will be pleasantly surprised. It's another sign of a great leader: knowing when to step in, and knowing when to stay out of the way.

7. Don't give up. Self-explanatory, but so critical. If you stay in business long enough, things will get tough for you and your team at some point. If things are real bad, you might be the only one who's willing to stay with it, but stay with it you must. Your team will be watching you. If you show signs of giving up, they almost certainly will, too. But if you show courage, faith in the business, a willingness to never quit, most will join with you. Everyone will take their cue from you. Show them your resolve. Remember, you never fail until you quit.

PRINCIPLE 2

The first entrepreneurial lesson from the military: it's not about you, it's about others first. Think of others—your family, your employees, your clients—before yourself.

CHAPTER FORTY-ONE

Can You Take Advice From a Teenager?

"Wisdom can come from almost anywhere and almost anyone, but will you recognize and use it?"

RECENTLY, I HAD THE great privilege of witnessing the first-ever high school graduating class of the Virginia Academy in Ashburn, Virginia. It's a private Christian school and was experiencing good growth and great success by its high school students, evidenced by the very high percentage of students accepted to college. They also had many students awarded full academic scholarships and a basketball scholarship offered to one of their student athletes to Vanderbilt University. It was quite impressive for a relative private-school newcomer.

During the graduation ceremony, it's customary to give the salutatorian (the student with the second-highest grade point average) the honor of addressing the class, parents, and faculty. Normally these speeches tend to be clever and funny, meant to get a response from the students. Safe to say, if I were giving the speech to my fellow classmates, I would definitely go for the humorous versus the profound. But when the class salutatorian, Nicholas Mets, rose to give his speech, he did briefly venture into the humorous but then turned serious and said something that really impressed me, so much so that months later, I'm still thinking about it.

The Teenager Speaks

Nicholas mentioned how things had been challenging for him during his recent school years, but through the encouragement of caring teachers, counselors, and coaches, he not only properly completed his coursework but finished strong enough to be standing there as the salutatorian. He said he learned many things along the way and highlighted them during his speech.

Nicholas finished by summing up his high school experience, stating, "If it doesn't challenge you, it doesn't change you." Wow! I said to my wife sitting next me, "What a great thought!" Afterward, I went up to Nicholas and congratulated him and said he had given me wise advice and I appreciated it. He looked a bit surprised, me being a much older man, not believing he could say anything of use to me. So I repeated myself. He smiled and said, "You're welcome!" A great response, actually.

I love Nicholas' statement. As I see it, it implies a couple things worth considering:

1. Any cause (project, goal, personal growth effort) you accept and strive to attain must be something beyond your own capability or you will not grow. Setting a goal that you can already attain is, well, underwhelming, unimpressive, and unworthy of your effort. You can't change the world or grow to become a greater version of yourself unless you reach beyond where you already are. Allow yourself to go beyond your current self by getting out of your comfort zone, embracing the sometimes messy and confusing world of all that is new. As is often said, "Nothing ventured, nothing gained."

2. Whatever becomes your cause is worth doing well. Strive for excellence, not perfection. I recently saw a very inspiring commercial for athletic gear where several athletes were shown looking totally exhausted, dripping with sweat, but each somehow picked themselves up and said, "Just one more." Each athlete made one more effort, to run one more lap, lift one more rep on the barbell, attempt the high jump one more time, try one more pole vault, even while completely out of gas, digging deep to try just a little harder in hopes of attaining their respective goals. They were willing to pay the extra price to succeed. Whatever you do in life, whatever cause you fight for, if it is worth doing, it is worth doing well with all your might, giving it your best.

The Professor Speaks

My beloved deceased uncle, Dr. John York, a lifelong missionary to Nigeria and the surrounding nations of West Africa, was a devoted Christian and educator. He established a fully accredited university program there, offering degrees from bachelors all the way up to PhD. It took a long time to achieve, practically his whole professional life. When we talked, he would often challenge me by asking about my life goals—not the everyday routine goals, but the real lifelong goals that take a devoted effort to achieve and become your purpose in life.

One time when I told him some of my goals, Uncle John responded, "But that sounds like something you could do right now with your current knowledge and your own resources." He would then say, "If your life goals are fully achievable by you alone, then I question whether that is what you were really created to do. But if your goals are beyond just you and require the help of others—friends, family, associates, as well as God's help—then I think you're much closer to finding your intended purpose in life. We often underreach in our purpose and lose the opportunity for real change in our lives and the lives of others."

Wow, again! He got me with that.

My uncle John lived what he taught, too. His lifelong ambition to establish a fully accredited seminary in Nigeria was way beyond just him alone. Because of his vision, looking beyond just his own strength and resources, thousands of men and women in Nigeria today have earned degrees of every kind and are living fulfilled, purposeful lives, helping their fellow man. My uncle John was taken from us after a long bout with leukemia, but his legacy lives on in Nigeria each semester when they graduate more and more students equipped to change lives.

My uncle John and Nicholas—one a vastly experienced, wise, and educated man, and the other an eighteen-year-old recent high school graduate—have both given me extremely valuable words of wisdom. We all seek wisdom, but you can find it in places or from people you wouldn't normally expect. Most people would stop and listen to my uncle, but how many would stop and listen to Nicholas? I understand why. But we should all keep our minds open, our eyes and ears open, and our options open so that we do not miss real wisdom when it presents itself. You never know from where it's going to come.

What are your goals? What causes will you work for? Do they require you to change? If not, Nicholas would say to look higher. Can you do them alone without any help? Uncle John would say to look higher. Are you aiming high enough?

PRINCIPLE 3

We all seek wisdom, but it can come from unexpected places or from unexpected people. Keep your eyes, ears, and mind open. You never know from where it will come.

CHAPTER FORTY-TWO

Never Be Impressed With Yourself

"Pride goes before destruction,
and a haughty spirit before a fall."
—Proverbs

THERE ARE MANY OBSTACLES for the small business owner and entrepreneur. Many are professional: competition, weakening demand for your product or service, employee challenges, lack of sufficient resources, changing market conditions, and so on. But other obstacles are more personal and attack from the inside: fear of failure, lack of self-confidence, distractions brought on by troubles at home or in your personal life, jealousy of another's success, greed, and so forth.

But one inside or personal thing that often creeps into the picture gradually, especially when you've achieved some success, is pride—the bad kind. I know you've seen this kind of pride before. Think of a Hollywood actor or actress, or a professional athlete you've seen on television who seems to talk only about themselves. As they spoke, it became obvious they were very impressed with themselves, and if you're like me, maybe your face began to scrunch up as if you'd eaten a very sour lemon. It was distasteful to hear and watch that famous person talk about how wonderful they are.

On the other hand, if you've ever watched a famous personality on television who was not self-centered, listened to them brag about their coworkers or teammates or give credit to God for their success, you probably found yourself smiling as they spoke. Very pleasant and heartwarming to watch. You might have even felt your eyes well up with tears as they spoke of a loved one to whom they owed their success. This was much more pleasant that the haughty, prideful person, wasn't it?

I do believe in having confidence in yourself, knowing your abilities, your successes, and having pride (the good kind) in your work and your team. But there's a big difference in that kind of pride and the kind that makes your face scrunch up when you hear unsavory comments. So what is the problem with the bad kind of pride? What kind of harm can it do? Why should I concern myself with it? Let me lay out some things below I've observed with the wrong kind of pride and what its impact can be.

1. <u>It lessens trust</u>. If you have the wrong kind of pride, people who have to work with you will likely begin to trust you less. They will think that you will act in your own interests first, not those of the team or organization. They'll believe you think it's all about you. Lack of trust also tends to cause division, and that's the death knell to a team. It will never reach its potential if divided.

2. <u>It lowers morale</u>. When you have less trust, the work is less fun and morale greatly suffers. People around you won't look optimistically at their futures. Hope will suffer, and where there is no hope, people will see no reason to continue to work hard. They will feel less valued, and depressed about their jobs.

3. <u>It does not promote team or collaboration</u>. Since everyone believes you're all about yourself only, the team culture suffers.

The word *team* is not in the working vocabulary of your organizational lexicon. People will feel their thoughts or ideas will be dismissed, that only you are allowed to have a good idea. Your team will consist of many functioning parts rather than one cohesive unit.

4. It obscures your vision. You will only see things from your perspective, oblivious to others and their feelings or ideas. You will therefore have a singular vision, losing the multidimensional benefits you get when you open your mind to a variety of perspectives and experiences. Your business or project is now in real jeopardy, racing down the road to failure.

5. It is distasteful to all those around you. The very thing you find so wonderful—you, the person—others will find repugnant. Sadly, you may not even realize it. If you want to be liked, you must consider doing a 180-degree turn.

• • •

If you're one of the distastefully prideful people, any advice I now give to change your course will likely be dismissed. But here goes, anyway. What it all comes down to is character, who you really are as a person. My advice is as follows:

1. When something goes wonderfully in your work or project, be quick to share the credit with everyone. Let someone else toot your horn; never do it yourself. When you toot your horn, it's like biting down on a fresh, juicy lemon to everyone else. Ugh! Very sour.

2. When something goes really wrong, be quick to take the blame. Never point the finger. Take responsibility, even if you weren't anywhere near the mistake or error. Your leadership

and character will show more when bad things are happening than when good things are happening.

3. Praise in public, give personal feedback in private. When someone does great, tell everyone openly. When someone makes an error, pull them aside privately and discuss it, without emotion or blame, but as someone who cares for them and wants to see them improve and excel.

These three acts of selflessness will endear everyone to you, strengthen your team, and build trust. As the business owner or entrepreneur, you need people who are devoted to you, the person, as well as your business. Reject the wrong kind of pride, in everything you do. In this way, you fortify your character and increase your chances for success, stronger relationships, and real happiness.

PRINCIPLE 4

Never be too impressed with yourself, leading with humility. Be quick to share the credit for success and take the blame for failure.

Part Six Recap: More Wisdom and Insights

PRINCIPLE 1

The more you know, the more you realize you how little you know. This is the beginning of wisdom. Let this inform your future.

PRINCIPLE 2

The first entrepreneurial lesson from the military: it's not about you, it's about others first. Think of others—your family, your employees, your clients—before yourself.

PRINCIPLE 3

We all seek wisdom, but it can come from unexpected places or from unexpected people. Keep your eyes, ears, and mind open. You never know from where it will come.

PRINCIPLE 4

Never be too impressed with yourself, leading with humility. Be quick to share the credit for success, and take the blame for failure.

PART SEVEN:

EPILOGUE

CHAPTER FORTY-THREE

Final Thoughts on Overcoming

We've reached the last chapter of this book. What I'd like to do now is give you an update on my situation because I think you might be wondering, "So, what happened, Wayland? How have things gone for you?" Then I want to close with some final thoughts on overcoming in business and life.

What's Happened Since the Downturn, Wayland?

I'm happy to report that my situation is great and getting better. I can honestly say I've recovered from my tragic saga, emotionally and financially. Since the downturn in my business, which began in 2010, I've been tremendously blessed.

1. My wife and I are still very much in love having celebrated our forty-second wedding anniversary.
2. My son Chris married a lovely woman, Christiana. I love her dearly. She is like my own daughter. They have given us three granddaughters, Kinley, Harlie, and Callie, and a grandson, Cade, who I love more than life itself. They have wonderfully changed my life completely.

3. My daughter, Lynnsey, married a wonderful young man, Michael. We love him very much. He is like my own son, and he's so fun to be around. They have given us a beautiful granddaughter named Grace whom I also love more than life itself. She has brought such joy.

4. My son Nick has a college degree and is an aspiring musician. He's preparing for a major career upgrade, and I'm very proud of him.

5. My non-US business more than tripled in the years following, providing me with a good income. I had the best team of employees I've ever had—a real dream team. At the risk of sounding mushy, I must say that I loved that team. They were so fun to be around. They were led by two amazing young men, Richard and Dave. Their chemistry, integrity, and leadership were second to none. Our number of clients increased, and they were each raving fans of our team and its capabilities. For a number of reasons, I did decide to close the business as COVID-19 hit the US, and in retrospect that proved to be a wise decision.

6. Our personal financial situation has completely recovered. In fact, Karen and I reentered the home-buying market, purchasing a beautiful home.

7. My parents suffered severe health problems, incurring huge medical bills and expenses. They are both fine now. But I was happy and honored to be able to pay their bills and take care of them because of my business's recovery. Being able to take care of my family is very important to me, which is why I have listed this event here as a "win."

8. Finally, I've moved on to a new phase of my professional life. As I watched COVID-19 cause tremendous problems

> in our national medical/pharmaceutical supply chain, I felt compelled to "come off the bench" and try to lend a hand where I could. I was hired by a firm who had a contract with the Department of Health & Human Services in Washington, DC. I joined a fantastic team of experts with the mission of saving lives and protecting Americans in the arena of public health preparedness and response. Since joining this team, I have spent most of my time and effort in the fight against COVID-19. It has been a wonderfully purposeful experience for me. I am enjoying it very much and hope to be a member of this team for a long time, helping our nation prepare for the next public health crisis.

Of course, not everything went well during our recovery. There were many bad days, life challenges, and mountains to climb. Sometimes I was discouraged, thinking our lives would never return to normal. Karen and I just kept focusing ahead, putting one foot in front of the other. Some days all we could do was show up, no fanfare, no cheering fans, no joy, no feeling of conquering or overcoming. However, I think sometimes just showing up is a win. Keeping yourself on track, on target, each day is a win. Doing the right thing, when no one notices or is watching, is a win. Loving and being loved is a win. Helping a neighbor, expecting nothing in return, is a win. Working in anonymity, each day, consistently, with purpose, is a huge win. Not letting your circumstances define who you are is a win. And if you string enough wins together, you start to overcome!

Thoughts on Overcoming

Merriam-Webster's dictionary defines an *overcomer* as "one who succeeds in dealing with or gaining control of some problem or difficulty." I especially identify with the words "one who succeeds in . . . gaining control." To me, the "gaining" is key. This implies repeated effort—not quitting or failing, but trying and trying again until control is "gained." It's a process. How long it takes, no one can know. It's different for everyone. But if you keep showing up, every day, you will gain control and eventually overcome.

Since this book is a playbook, and I like lists, let me give you my thoughts on what an overcomer looks like, in no particular order. Look at these characteristics and decide which ones you do well, which ones you don't do well, and which ones you don't do at all. Take what's useful and cast the rest aside.

1. An overcomer knows who he or she is. Their identity is not in their work or position but in who they are as a person. For example, I consider myself a consensus builder, an influencer, someone who can communicate ideas well, persuading others to seriously consider them. My identity is not in my college degrees, my certifications, the material things I own, the positions I hold or have held, but in who I am. What I hope my family and friends say about me is "He's a good friend, a good listener, a good communicator, a compassionate heart, an honest man, a family man." I don't want the first thing someone says about me to be, "Oh, he's a business owner, an MBA, a retired naval officer, owns two houses," and so on. Do you see my point? Overcomers have higher aspirations, higher goals, and higher thoughts. Purpose and meaning far outweigh titles and things in the mind of an overcomer.

2. Overcomers believe in themselves. This is not to say they don't have days where they are completely depressed or deflated about themselves or their situations. Not at all. But in the final analysis, they believe they can overcome. They hold on to hope. They don't let circumstances, failures, or others define who they are. They know their weaknesses and strive to improve in those areas. They also know their strengths and strive to take advantage of them. They also believe in their purpose

or calling. This keeps them going in hard times. People can suffer many things if they have hope and know their purpose.

3. Overcomers have the courage to act. If you are going to overcome anything, you will have to act, to do something. You can't just crawl into a hole and wait for success to find you. You have get out there and work, making an effort. Sometimes you have to take calculated risks. This takes courage. I like what Senator John McCain said about courage in his book: "Courage is not the absence of fear, but the capability to act despite our fears." To me, this means sometimes you have to step out, even though you might be nervous, even trembling out of fear. Sometimes, even after I've done all my due diligence and the obvious answer is to move forward with a business decision, when I actually have to step out, sign the document, and make the call, I still feel the fear. Overcomers have the courage to do what they know is right, what they know is best and gives them the best chance for success. They can push through the fear. They aren't foolish, but they have the courage to act.

4. Overcomers gain wisdom from failures, making it part of their next steps to success. Their mindset is "I'm either learning, or winning. I never lose unless I quit."

5. Overcomers seek wise counsel. They know they don't know it all or have all the answers. They have mentors they meet with regularly. These mentors care about them and hold them accountable for agreed goals and targets, personal and professional. They have permission to speak into the overcomer's life, to tell the brutal truth when needed, or to pat them on the back when deserved.

6. Overcomers have healthy priorities. When I was aboard the USS *Mars* in the Persian Gulf, just hours before the ground war was to begin in Operation Desert Storm, I remember

thinking that my life and the lives of our crew could be in grave danger very soon. Reports predicting tens of thousands of casualties on the US side were being thrown around in the news. I was worried. Already two ships nearby had been hit by mines, causing human casualties and serious damage. We were preparing the ship to respond to missile attacks, mines, possible fire and flooding. I saw nervousness and fear in the eyes of my division.

The reason I'm telling you this story? During these sobering hours before hostilities were to begin, I had only three concerns: (1) my faith in God—I had made peace with Him; (2) my family—their welfare, and how would they survive if I died in this war; and (3) my duty—whether I was ready to defend this ship and its crew. Every other worry or concern I might have had fell off the radar of my mind. If it wasn't those top three things, it wasn't important. I gave it no further thought.

Here's the point: war has a way of clarifying things, helping you see what's really important. If these three things really are what's important in war, aren't they just as important regardless of the situation—in everyday life, for example? The answer is a resounding, "Yes!" The problem is that life often rears its ugly head and confuses the picture, jumbles the priorities, and the most important priorities get diluted or weakened with other less important priorities. Overcomers regularly examine their priorities to make sure they keep the top priorities in their proper place.

7. <u>Overcomers have a solid personal support system of family, friends, and associates; they cultivate and protect it to keep it that way</u>. When trouble comes, their support system is there for them, helping them keep things in perspective, to see things clearly, and to support them through difficulty. They

are also there to help them celebrate the good times in life, too. An overcomer gives as much to his support system as they receive. An overcomer's most important relationships are in this system. This is their community, which we all need.

8. Overcomers develop and maintain good habits. They make it a habit to eat properly, get adequate rest, exercise regularly, keep a daily journal, read good books, give of themselves and their resources, enjoy culture and art, limit television and smartphone time, take breaks and holidays, are slow to anger, are quick to be kind, are people of principle, live with honor and integrity, do the right thing when no one is watching, and are quick to share the credit for wins and accept the blame for losses.

Looking at the list above, I freely admit I'm still working on these things myself. I don't have them all mastered. I don't think you'll ever "arrive" and be done with it. Overcoming is a lifelong journey, but well worth it. I think life should be less about how long you live and more about what you did with the time you were given. Overcomers make the most of every day, living life to the fullest.

It is my hope that this book has challenged your thinking. If you are a struggling business owner, I hope it has given you hope and reason to believe in yourself and your business again. If you are thinking about going into business, I hope this book eases your way into the most professionally exciting thing anyone can do—own a successful business. At some point, we will all go through difficulty. When you do, my prayer is that you are now better prepared to be an overcomer in business and life.

APPENDIX A:

COMPLETE LIST OF ALL PRINCIPLES

Part One Recap: How Do You Think?

PRINCIPLE 1

Your business and life are interdependent, one affecting the other, and must be kept in balance.

PRINCIPLE 2

Your ideas are powerful. Make sure they have what they need to succeed.

PRINCIPLE 3

Make sure you understand the question or problem and are thinking correctly about it. If you don't identify the right question, you will answer the wrong one.

PRINCIPLE 4

What you believe about yourself and your situation will drive your decisions, and your decisions determine your outcomes. Change your beliefs to change your decisions and thereby your outcomes.

PRINCIPLE 5

If you haven't already found your purpose, begin an unforced journey of discovery. Allow your purpose to emerge in an honest way. Then let your purpose set your course in life. Be willing to change course as conditions change.

PRINCIPLE 6

Let your goals and purpose influence your major decisions, not your worries, challenges, fears, setbacks, disgruntled employees, or problems at home. And take the time the decision deserves.

Part Two Recap: The Top Things I Wish I'd Known Before Starting My Business

PRINCIPLE 1

When we focus on nothing else but pursuing the dream, leaving all else aside, we do serious harm to ourselves and those we love and care deeply about. It is critical that you maintain a balance between your personal and business lives.

PRINCIPLE 2

Don't buy it unless you need it. If you need it, don't hesitate to buy it. But make sure you need it. Be honest with yourself. And avoid debt like the plague. Use your own resources first.

PRINCIPLE 3

It's not a matter of *if* things will go wrong, but *when*. Remove uncertainty and discover more about your business, market, and customer through planning, creating responses to likely scenarios you may face in business. Ensure you include margin for error.

PRINCIPLE 4

When considering debt, be honest and ask yourself hard questions. Consider whether it's good debt or bad debt—will it increase your income or worth? If not, avoid it like the plague.

PRINCIPLE 5

Your relationships and relationship skills are *more* critical than your business skills. Cultivate and improve them to ensure sustained success and happiness—in life and business.

PRINCIPLE 6

Learn and practice good business practices and life principles. If you truly do what's right for your business and life every day, based on proven practices and principles, you will be ready for most any challenge that comes.

PRINCIPLE 7

Employee skills can be developed. Character cannot. Make every effort to hire well. Take the time it deserves because it's essential to get it right.

PRINCIPLE 8

Give your important decisions time to mature. Quiet yourself and listen. Let peace be your umpire.

PRINCIPLE 9

No one person can know it all. Stay teachable. Practice a healthy humility. Listen to understand, not to respond.

PRINCIPLE 10

Identify your possible exit points *before* entering into any significant contract or business relationship. The best time to find a way out of a bad situation is *not* when you are already in it.

Part Three Recap: Hard-Won Business Lessons That Work

PRINCIPLE 1

A business partnership can be just like a marriage, either the best or worst thing ever invented in life. Take care who you choose. Strive to maintain fairness for a lasting partnership.

PRINCIPLE 2

Often, the best strategy during difficult times is to do nothing. Consider whether any action is required at all. Moving too quickly can make things worse. Don't fix something that isn't broken.

PRINCIPLE 3

Stop doing what's not working, and do more of what is working. Prune those activities that do not contribute to your core business. Get a mentor to advise you.

PRINCIPLE 4

Don't delay tough employee decisions. The welfare of the company and its current employees must come first. Plus, delays do yourself and the employee a great disservice.

PRINCIPLE 5

HALT! Delay the big decisions until you are at your best, not hungry, angry, lonely, or tired.

PRINCIPLE 6

Establish and maintain your credibility. Guard it at all times. As King Solomon the wise once said, "A good name is rather to be had than great riches."

PRINCIPLE 7

Mitigate the risk to your startup business with strategies to conserve your cash and limit your financial exposure should things go wrong.

PRINCIPLE 8

When considering a new offering, there is a big difference between taking a calculated risk and gambling with your business. Don't gamble.

Part Four Recap: Hard-Won Life Lessons That Work

PRINCIPLE 1

In a conflict, the goal should be to find a way to resolve differences and move forward, for the good of everyone—*not* to win the argument.

PRINCIPLE 2

To be able to operate at your best and highest, your life-giving relationships need to be strong, happy, and healthy. Make them your highest priority.

PRINCIPLE 3

Regularly journal your thoughts, feelings, and concerns to disentangle your mind and ease the worries of life and business.

PRINCIPLE 4

Make it a point to enjoy the journey, not just the destination. You will enjoy your life more and increase your happiness.

PRINCIPLE 5

Your life is like a checking account. Taking care of yourself is like making a deposit, whereas work is like a withdrawal. Don't overdraw your account, because you can't give what you don't have. Keep a proper balance to be your best.

PRINCIPLE 6

Keep an attitude of gratitude, no matter what. The benefits are many and far-reaching.

PRINCIPLE 7

Entrepreneurs are prone to work overload. Regularly assess yourself. Take immediate steps to correct an imbalance, in your life and business.

PRINCIPLE 8

Think of limitations not as a constraint but as a gift. Embrace and operate within them to achieve greater balance in life and business.

Part Five Recap: When It All Goes Wrong

PRINCIPLE 1

Forgive yourself for past failures and see the good in them. They are a stepping stone to wisdom, better judgment, and success. Now move forward and dream again.

PRINCIPLE 2

Character matters and will contribute to your fate in a crisis, for better or worse. Cultivate a strong character within yourself by doing the right thing all the time.

PRINCIPLE 3

When the storms of life and business toss you to and fro, don't fight the storm with drastic actions. Keep it straight and level, and you will come through it.

PRINCIPLE 4

Stay teachable, always learning and growing with an open mind. You cannot take your business beyond where you are.

PRINCIPLE 5

Setbacks are not permanent and do not define you. Change your mind. Make your setback part of your next success.

PRINCIPLE 6

You can learn as much or more from poor leaders as good ones. Let them show you how *not* to do things. It can be very valuable and inform your future as a leader.

Part Six Recap: More Wisdom and Insights

PRINCIPLE 1

The more you know, the more you realize you how little you know. This is the beginning of wisdom. Let this inform your future.

PRINCIPLE 2

The first entrepreneurial lesson from the military: it's not about you, it's about others first. Think of others—your family, your employees, your clients—before yourself.

PRINCIPLE 3

We all seek wisdom, but it can come from unexpected places or from unexpected people. Keep your eyes, ears, and mind open. You never know from where it will come.

PRINCIPLE 4

Never be too impressed with yourself, leading with humility. Be quick to share the credit for success and take the blame for failure.